THE

TRUTH

ABOUT

HAPPINESS

Exchanging The Falsehood Of Happiness
For Christ's Lasting Joy

By J.E. Berry

Additional references in the rear.

<u>Dedications</u>

To the God who called and equips me.

To the husband who loves and encourages me.

To the mother who edifies me.

To my children who energize me.

To the family and friends who embrace me.

To you who God loves and adores

Special Thanks

Angel Lewis

Dwana Murphy

Regan Blanchard

RaShonda Jordan

Marion Sanford

Brittni Landry

Laura Nichols

Thank you so very much for your servant hearts!

Forward

"In J.E.'s book, The Truth About Happiness, she delivers fresh new insights into challenges all Christians face. Told with a down to earth style and plenty of humor, this book will inspire and encourage readers to take a deeper look into their spiritual lives and to follow the path towards true happiness." - *Dana Mentink*, Author (Multi published, award winning writer of Christian fiction [Author of 20 Harlequin Books], www.danamentink.com)

"Oh happiness, how we chase you incessantly! J.E. Berry has hit a home run with her in-depth exploration into that elusive topic of happiness, why we chase it, and how we can find something far deeper - true joy. This is a page-turner for all Christians as we seek to go deeper in our walk with our Savior. Kudos J.E. Berry!"
- *Jennifer Maggio*, (CEO/Founder of *The Life of A Single Mom* Ministries, Author of *The Church and the Single Mom* and 3 other titles, thelifeofasinglemom.com)

"If you're looking for truth that's written in a nononsense kind of way, then this is the book for you. J.E. understands the nitty, gritty of everyday life. With honesty and humility, she insightfully weaves scripture into your real life challenges...all the while making you feel like you're sitting down for coffee with a good friend."
- *Andrea Coli,* Writer/Speaker (Author of *Scriptless: What I Learned About God on the Las Vegas Strip,* Andreacolispeaks.com *)*

"As Christians we are constantly in need of being reminded of the biblical principles for living. J.E. puts before us a treasure chest of truth right at our fingertips."
- *Kevin Gordon*
(Founder/President of *Vallejo Bible College, vallejobiblecollege.org)*

"J. E. Berry takes a three-pronged approach to help us experience true joy verses temporal happiness. Hope for our stories starts with a humble, transparent look at her own story that allows us to know we are not alone. She gives practical, inspiring exercises to allow us to find God and His joy in the midst of our heart wrestlings. Finally, she speaks to the need in all of us to know peace and contentment in our mind and soul that can only be found in an active relationship with

God. This book is a must on my shelf and to point others to a life of joy with God and with others."

- *Joan Gallagher,* Author/Speaker (*Women Mentoring Women*, Contributing blogger for *Sweet Jesus Ministries*, *Bible Gateway* blogger, joangallagher.net)

"The Truth About Happiness" conveys a rich, transparent, and thought provoking message to enhance us all. It is compelling to the Christian on their Christ like journey and justly practical enough to lead the lost to salvation. What better interpretation to offer, of how to live maximally, than one built solely on evidence through Scripture. Sensational read!"
- *LaToya R. Braxton*, M.Ed.,Ed.S.,
(MFTI: Clinical Mental Health Counselor, ACA, Association for Creativity in Counseling, founder of COVEREDGIRL, Incorporated [coveredgirl.org])

"I found this book to be a very thought provoking book. It encouraged me to believe that no matter what I deal with in life I can find true happiness with Jesus Christ. It challenges you to look beyond your circumstance and to pursue what is needed through God's word to change your way of thinking into positive thinking; in doing so the end result will be true happiness, which is "THE JOY OF OUR LORD JESUS CHRIST". I was encouraged and hope that whoever reads this book will be encouraged also." - *Millicent Williams* (Board Member of *California Women's Retreat, cawr.org*)

TABLE OF CONTENTS

INTRO

Before we move any further, let's pray together.

Lord Jesus, thank You so very much for bringing us together on this journey. Lord, we ask that You would come and meet us here. God, we need You to show us the truth through Your eyes. We surrender to You our expectations and our desires today. Help us to reach out to You and to grab on to You tightly. Let this book bring You glory and let our lives be changed to align with Your image. Thank You, God, for all that You are. In Jesus name, AMEN!

OK Friend, you and I are about to embark on a very personal journey together. But first I feel the need to throw out a quick disclaimer. So here it is. This is not a self-help book with "5 easy ways to find joy". This book will challenge us to re-evaluate, re-shape, and re-align our thinking with God's truth. Together we will push past what we know about happiness to live freed by the truth of Scripture and in the gift of joy that has been so graciously given to us. We are going to get uncomfortable, vulnerable, and probably a little emotional on this journey. So I find it very fitting that I introduce myself to you and let you get a look into the life of your new friend.

Where do I start? I'm a wife, a mother of five, a speaker, a writer, a friend, a worshiper, a wanderer, a launderer, a short order chef and the list goes on. In order to properly introduce myself to you I have to show you a small portion of what all of me looks like in full outer ring circumference before we dive deep into the foggy waters and messy puddles that fill my very God chiseled testimony. Stepping out of my comfort zone and into trusting my Father has led me to this very page. This season of my journey reflects the places God has brought me from and the grace of Christ that brought me through each testimony. As a speaker and writer, I make every effort to surrender my agenda to the Lord and allow Him to use what He has done in my life to teach His infallible word to His people. All the while He is teaching my heart in the same instance.

Being a wanderer at heart, my story is a culmination of statistics, heartbreak, a fight to control, God's unrelenting love and His sweet and tender grace. In my life, I had done a great job trying to forget the not so fuzzy memories in my past. Even still today I fight with the shame that tries to leach onto me when I recall some of the horrific choices I made as a wounded, wandering soul. I had gotten really good at hiding behind my smile and strong exterior but eventually I realized that all the wounds of my past were still wide open and bleeding profusely. All the band-aids I was putting over them just were not sufficient.

A product of divorce and a child of a former addict, I saw and heard a lot of things that I would never want my own children to. Things that I thought were perfectly normal until I was an adult. Even though I have always had a great relationship with both my parents, it was not a "normal" family setting. I can still recall hearing yelling in my home that caused me to curl up in my bed and hum myself to sleep. The day my parents split, my life changed forever. At the young age of 12, I began to live a double life as I tried to be two different girls every week as I adjusted to my environments, all while pretending to be "OK" and unaffected by the major life altering circumstances.

In my brain I figured that if I ignored it all, it would not be a factor. So I masked everything in a smile, caricature happiness and "no big deal" attitude. I spent most of my early adult years trying to be in control of everything in my life so that I could be "happy". I had the brilliant idea that I could actually make myself happy. Being in "control" was my way of not making the same mistakes that my parents and other family members had made. All the while, I was actually and making equally damaging mistakes that left even bigger wounds than I already had. In my pea brain, I had set in stone that I would control my body and everything that I did. No one would tell me what to do or how to do it. I just wanted so much to avoid being in an unfulfilling marriage or lead a life that was destroyed by other people. The result was promiscuity, unplanned pregnancy, depression, anger and fear.

All of this was masked in "Sunday Christianity" and a smile. There were times I wondered if anyone knew how I really felt or if they would even care. See, I was the one that everyone else came to for advice. I was the one who tried to hold up the blood stained banner in my circle of friends all while shaming it as I lived a life buried in sin. I was a complete mess wrapped in denial.

While still trying to climb out of that mess, I married the love of my life and God rescued me from my pit. It was a long walk out of the abyss that I had dug for myself but God was faithful to finish what He began in me. He began to show me what joy really looks like and who is really in control so that I could stop trying to do a job I wasn't qualified to do. Shortly after the wedding, the Lord called me to write. My answer to His call came at a snail crawl but I finally jumped over fear and ran to Him with anticipation. However, the more I ran toward Jesus, the more the enemy chased me with the very fear I had hurdled to be obedient.

Fear was like that last piece of lint on a black shirt that just wouldn't come off. I was fighting it tooth and nail as I attempted to be the "perfect" wife and mother. It crippled me and made me not want to do anything let alone step out in faith toward what God called me to do. Thank God for deliverance! God delivered me from that crippling fear and has given me the strength and courage I need to walk out the vision He has for me. In this season, God has given me a heart to walk along side His people as they find joy in Him. This book is a journey from "happiness" to God's lasting "JOY". Together we will walk a revealing journey to dispel the lies we believe about happiness and find what real joy looks like when we drink from the never ending well of Jesus.

The truth is that we are all explorers on a journey to find out who we are and where we are going. My heart is to hold the hand of another, as we walk the journey together, looking the Father in the face.

The Start
of the Journey

Sooooo......

Late one night, when I was enjoying some one-onone quality time with my awesome husband, a thought went through my mind, "I am so happy." Along with that came other thoughts. "Why was I so unhappy before?" "Why are so many people not happy?" and "What makes us so unhappy in the first place?" Not to say that this moment is what my life is like on a 24hour basis. Naturally I have the not so happy moments like everyone else. However, these thoughts kind of made me sad for the people in my life who are living a not so happy life on a consistent basis with no hope for a happier day tomorrow. I have totally been in their shoes before. Giving myself all the pity parties that I could find excuses to decorate them with. Feeling completely hopeless, destitute and isolated. I recollect feeling all alone no matter how many people were surrounding me. Plus, of course, there was no one who knew what I was going through out of seven billion people on this earth. Back then I had the "maybe when" kind of thinking rather than the "why not now" kind of thinking. You know that thinking where you say to yourself, "Maybe when I get married I will really be happy." Or "Maybe when I finally move into my new house I will be satisfied." When the reality is that no external thing or form of human attempted solution can fill that void, even though we sometimes get caught up in the imagery of the falsehood of these things and believe the lies they're selling.

While, sitting with my husband that night I started to try and figure out in my head what I could say to my beloved friends and family, who seemed so unhappy and disheveled, to snap them out of whatever trance they were in and make them really start living the life God has for them. Besides, I have certainly seen that side of the dark and my heart simply broke for them that night. I thought, maybe if I just figure the right way to say something or recommend a book of some sort or buy them a card then maybe, just maybe they would start to head towards the light. Then I realized that these people are the only ones who can start the transformations in their lives.

I remembered that there was a point in my own life when I saw that there was nothing I could produce that would bring me the happiness that I was looking for. That the satisfaction I was looking for had been stirring in me by the God who saved me, waiting to be partaken of by the one who had inherited it. ME. It was the fruit of *JOY* that I had yet to eat of because I was choosing to seek the bargain basement version, happiness. It was up to me to choose the joy that had been bought for me on the cross. And, just like in my circumstance, my loved ones, and you, are the only ones who can make the choice to say; "I'm ready to have joy now." We must surrender the junk in our lives that is keeping us from experiencing God's lasting joy, accepting the one thing in this life that can bring true happiness, Jesus.

We can't chose joy for someone else anymore than we can chose salvation for them.

This realization also made me see that unfortunately, it may take years, if ever, for some people to see the truth that their happiness is found in a choice they may have yet to make. No matter how much advice I give or prayers I say, if they don't chose to follow the path that will set them free, their hearts will remain heavy. My life before becoming completely sold out for Christ was a lot like this. I had yet to make a real decision concerning my walk with Christ. I was just kind of hanging on a dead branch praying it didn't snap. Though I knew that I should turn to God's word, I procrastinated and postponed the choice to move forward in God's will. It's like I was afraid that I would loose something. Lord knows I needed to! I needed to loose everything I had conned myself into believing was meant for me when it was totally going against God's perfect will. I needed to wake up and make the choice to pick up the cup of hope that had been poured for me. It's like giving a thirsty man a bucket of water but he refuses to drink it. God has given us the bucket so why aren't people drinking?

I'm sure you know someone in this type of rut or maybe it's you. Maybe today you are like me and just want to figure out how to stand in front of the joy stealer and say "NO!"

The comforting truth I have come to embrace along this journey is, we all struggle with making the choice to see the bright light. Whether it be a daily struggle or an every now and then type of struggle. We all come to a place where we are looking for some sunshine to break through and give us hope for a more pleasant life experience. I've also unveiled that the majority of the human race has a skewed view about what true happiness really looks like in the first place. Making it hard to grasp because we're reaching for the counterfeit instead. In this book, we are going to dive into some areas that are going to help us see where we can make choices that will help us find the authentic happiness we're actually looking for. Joy!

Discovering that the truth of the matter is that we can decide the fate of our life's joy meter is a little sobering. Who wants to think that the reason they aren't living a life of joy is because they chose not to? I mean really! However, in all honesty, when I think of moments when I am feeling a bit depressed or less than cheery, it's because of how I have chosen to react to whatever life is throwing me at the moment instead of choosing to access the gift of joy that comes free with salvation.

If you know someone who refuses to choose to go toward the light, just pray about their situation and let it go. I know it's frustrating to watch someone you love go off the deep end when they don't have to but sometimes they have to fall off the bed in order for them to wake up. So here I am releasing you from that burden.

If you are beginning this journey and aren't sure of where you stand in your salvation and relationship with the Father God, I pray that you stop for a moment and consider the opportunity to reconcile with your creator through Jesus Christ. I encourage you to turn to the reference section of this book and take a look at the plan of salvation and Scriptures referring to our redemption through Christ. Once you have done so, you will be fully equipped to receive all that God has for you as you embark on this journey.

Today is the day that we are going to choose to live in the Son light (you see what I did there) and make decisions that will help us remain there. I beg of you, do not finish this journey the same way you started. Allow God to work in your heart and transform you into the lighthearted free person He created you to be. Without bitterness, regret, shame, worthlessness, depression, sin, stress or strife. There is healing in the name of Jesus. All you have to do is call. *"Come to me, all you who are weary and burdened, and I will give you rest." Matthew 11:28 NIV.* Be encouraged to live **your** best Jesus centered life so that you can encourage others to do the same. Release the burdens and let's move forward. Now let's start our investigation!

Part 1

The Investigation

First….

Now that we're ready to get this show on the road, I want to share a little advice with you that will help you get the most out of this journey.

1. Pray, pray, pray, and pray some more.
2. This is your book, so write all over it.
3. Study the scriptures along the way and do your best to memorize the ones that stand out to you.
4. Journal what you are learning and discovering.
5. Don't allow fear to halt your journey, press through, you will be greatly rewarded.

6. If you can help it, don't walk this journey alone.

7. And most importantly, allow God to work in you.

Things you'll need for our journey:

- Pens/Highlighter
- Journal
- Bible and…
- A friend or friends

Here we GO!

"Happy" Meanings!

To begin my quest for the truth about happiness, I started with the simple stuff. I went right to the dictionary to look for some meanings. First let's examine the word *Happy*.

Happy: 1. a feeling of joy, pleasure, or good fortune. 2. Being especially well adapted. 3. Cheerful.

You will notice that none of these meanings say anything about having riches or material things. Unfortunately our society has mixed happiness with wealth and possessions. And then they wonder why millionaires are depressed and on the brink of jumping off a bridge. There is no material thing that can cause or bring true happiness to one's life. You will also notice that none of these definitions of the word "happy" are long lasting or permanent. Feelings are about as sifty as the sand of an hourglass and the term "being" is also pretty wobbly. All of these meanings can be disrupted by circumstance or change in emotions. Now, let's look at the word *Happiness*

Happiness: feeling or showing pleasure or contentment.

How unstable are these definitions? A state of being can be changed in the blink of an eye. Literally, a blink. If you get something in your eye, you go from comfortable to uncomfortable in a matter of a millisecond. Happiness can be easily disturbed by shifts of status, change in environment or temperature.

Our English interpretation of what it means to be happy or have joy has been poorly misconceived. Many of us have confused the truth about our happiness because of media, our surroundings, and what others have convinced us happiness consists of. We have given the job of making us happy to things (which can't take action in anyway without human interaction) or people that never signed up to do that job. We get married and think our spouse will make us happy. We have children and think that they will bring us satisfaction. We buy things, change jobs, change friends, change clothes and expect those things to finally fulfill our needs. This unfortunately has led to great confusion in not only adults but has bled confusion into our younger generations regarding the matter. Finding what true happiness looks like and where it comes from will help us to stop searching so hard for something intangible.

First we must realize that the truth about happiness is.......... that we aren't really looking for "happiness" in the first place. What we are really looking for is *JOY*, and not just typical run of the mill joy. The joy we are looking for has just one source, and it isn't us and it can't be purchased or produced. *"Then will I go to the altar of God, to God, <u>my joy and my delight."</u> Psalm 43:4*

This journey will be an unveiling of what joy is through Scripture. We will not look to the dictionary or our culture for the truth. We will look directly at the God's word and seek God's voice.

Truth?

Truth: **1. a.** Conformity to fact or actuality: *Does this story have any truth?* **b.** Reality; actuality: *In truth, he was not qualified for the job.* **c.** The reality of a situation: *The truth is, she respects your work.* **2. a.** A statement proven to be or accepted as true: *truths about nature.* **b.** Such statements considered as a group: *researchers in pursuit of truth.* **3.** Sincerity; integrity: *the truth of his intentions.*

The Bible declares that Jesus is the source of truth (John 14:6), not Darwin, and not CNN. Truth is another word in our vocabulary that has been redefined by the human race. We have confused opinions with truth. And have also replaced God's Word with the theories of the scientific world. I mean, come on, some of the theories sound a little loopy to even the simplest mind and still people are lured into believing some of the most ridiculous things that scientists have presented to us. But how can you blame them when the media is packed with all the crazy information that people come up with? With the connection that our society has the media, it's no wonder that the world is spiraling out of control. We must find real truth. Jesus! *"...I am the way, the **truth** and the life. No one can come to the father except through me" John 14:6*

If we don't even know what the truth is, it's a bit hard to figure out where we stand in the balance of our own lives. Knowing where we are spiritually and emotionally takes very in-depth and honest evaluation of self. Join me as we walk along and investigate a few things that are of great importance in our journey to joy.

Discovery #1-Who me?

It's a hard pill to swallow, but the reason most of us have not found true happiness/joy is because of ourselves. Somehow, when we think on all the things that have brought us to the place we are, a good portion of the negative submissions in our lives have (in our minds) happened because of someone else. For whatever reason, we find it hard to stop and look at the choices we have made stumbling blocks that we have put in front of ourselves or how we have chosen to respond to life's curveballs. For instance, if you get fired and are very angry and refuse to look for work, you have every right to blame the company you were fired from for why you are depressed, right? Wrong! We have control over how we react in every situation.

Yes it is unfortunate to lose employment but we are held accountable for our response. We have the option to look on the bright side and think to ourselves, "OK this is just where I am for now. It will get better and God is in control." It is much better for our emotional and mental health. If we make the decision that no one or nothing can steal our God given joy, no matter the circumstance, and take full responsibility for our reactions, joy could resonate no matter what you are going through. Joy is in the choice!

Choosing to live in the joy that God gives, changes the state of your happiness from temporal to a lasting state of joy that remains beyond current life circumstance.

Study Verse - Ecclesiastes 2:26 NKJV

"For to the one who pleases him God has given wisdom and knowledge and joy, but to the sinner he has given the business of gathering and collecting, only to give to one who pleases God. This also is vanity and a striving after wind."

Discovery #2- Saved?

Our walk with God can begin in many different circumstances: alone in a room, at an alter call or even in front of a grocery store. One thing remains the same for every Christian. We have all been delivered/saved. That being said, I believe that along our daily journey we can forget what it really means to be a Christian and what our future would be otherwise. Like the Israelites, *"They forgot the LORD their God, who had rescued them from all their enemies surrounding them." Judges 8:34 NLT.* Surely if we remembered these facts on a constant basis, we would have unspeakable joy all the time, striving to stay in the Lord's will. Just for the sake of clarification, we're going to take a closer look at the salvation we have been gifted. So, let's break down what we may be forgetting.

Why were we saved? Because God loved us so! *("For God so loved the world, that He gave His only begotten Son, that whoever should believe in Him should not perish, but have eternal life" John 3:16NASB)*

How were we saved? Through Christ's death and resurrection and upon our confession, acceptance of this gift and profession of faith. *("that if you confess with your mouth Jesus as Lord, and believe in your heart that God raised Him from the dead, you shall be saved; for with the heart the man believes, resulting in righteousness, and with the mouth he confesses, resulting in salvation. For the Scripture says, "Whoever*

believes in Him will not be disappointed." Romans
10:9-11.)

What were we saved from? Sin and the eternal death
that it results in. (*"For the <u>wages of sin is death</u>, but the
free gift of God is eternal life in Christ Jesus our Lord."*
*Romans 6:23, "It is a trustworthy statement, deserving
full acceptance, that Christ Jesus came into the world <u>to
save sinners</u>, among whom I am foremost of all."* 1
Timothy 1:15).

OK, now that we have that cleared up, join me in
looking at what it means to us. Across the board,
generally Christians are considered "saved " and that is
exactly what we have been. But today I have decided to
challenge that term and ponder adding another suitable
term for us that may be just as suited considering its
meaning. "Rescued" seems equally fitting, when we
take a look at how we come to Jesus. Let's look at a
couple definitions.

Saved: Keep safe or rescue (someone or something)
from harm or danger.

Rescued: Keep from being lost or abandoned;
<u>retrieve</u>.

Retrieve. What a great description of what the Lord
did for us on the cross. He retrieved us from the grips of
death. We were already headed to hell. He pulled us
right out of the fire. Oh where would we be if we had
not been rescued? *"But I trust in your unfailing love. I
will rejoice because you have <u>rescued</u> me."* Psalm 13:5
NLT. His unfailing love is what made our Father give

His own innocent child to be maimed, ridiculed, and killed to rescue a world of ungrateful sinners from an eternity in hell. Though it is our choice to be rescued, His unfailing love is always there, like a lighthouse guiding us to His rescue boat. His rescue boat built from the wood of the cross He hung on for us, waiting for us to jump in so that He can carry us to be reunited with the Father.

Life is tough sometimes and it can seem like the walls are caving in around us some days. In all the turmoil of life, our joy can be easily disrupted at times but there is lots of fuel to keep our joy lamp burning. Recall how little we have given up compared to what God has given for the sake of those who do or do not love Him. Recall how far you have come through Jesus. Recall where you could be. Recall how much He must love you to do what He did for you. And most of all recall being RESCUED, because the rescue is where your true life began. The moment you said "Jesus please come into my heart" you were rescued. Ladled out of the devil's wading pool, no longer drowning in sin and shame. Rescued from yourself, the world, and an eternity separated from our creator.

Unbelievable how we could ever forget. So in light of making better life choices, we should try our hardest to remember every day, that we have been rescued, how we were rescued and who was our *RESCUER. "He led me to a place of safety; he rescued me because he delights in me." 2 Samuel 22:20 NLT* **Discovery #3- Are we capable?**

Countless hours that we spend on this earth are dedicated to trying to satisfy one need or another within ourselves. Whether it is a need to be entertained or a need to be satisfied through appetite. We are so apt at attempting to satisfy ourselves that we are unaware that we are doing it for the most part. Our brains just function on a self-focused setting for majority of our life. Which is a shame because we have no idea what it takes to really satisfy ourselves, because we have not created ourselves. We don't know what our souls are hungry for. Only our Creator could possible know what would truly satisfy us because He designed us and He put the appetite in us that longs to be satisfied.

"Before I formed you in the womb I knew you, and before you were born I consecrated you; I appointed   you   a   prophet   to   the nations."   Jeremaiah 1:5

Our Father formed us, knows us, and ordained what we were created for. He knows what we need because He put us together. The same way an inventor knows his invention better than the person who uses it.

Our world runs on self-satisfaction. The reason is because we are all in need of satisfaction, and until our needs are met by the true Satisfier, we cannot know what it means to be truly satisfied.

"Blessed are those who hunger and thirst for righteousness,   for   they   shall   be satisfied."   Matthew 5:6

Discovery #4- Am I Partaking in the Fruit?

One thing I have struggled with, in my time as a human, has been learning that I am not the source of the goodness in my life. My flesh wants to be able to control the things that go on in my life and even the things not in my life. My humanistic instinct believes that it can do things that it can't. Things like, create an environment that will make me happy or "fix" the people around me. Thankfully we have a redeeming Father who was well prepared with a solution for the human condition. He sent His Son to solidify our salvation. Our salvation came with an added bonus, the Holy Spirit. The Spirit of Christ that dwells in the believer, His Spirit that guides and abides with us, the Spirit that produces fruit in the believer.

"And we are witnesses of these things; and so is the Holy Spirit, Whom God has given to those who obey Him."   Acts 5:32 NASB

"But I say, walk by the Spirit, and you will not carryout the desire of the flesh, For the flesh sets its desires against the Spirit, and the Spirit against the flesh; for these are in opposition to one another, so that you may not do the things that you please."
Galatians 5:16-17 NASB

The question is, was I or do I partake in the Spirit and all He offers to me? Or am I trying to do His job by attempting to guide myself? By trying to guide myself and direct my own life, I was actually being counterproductive. Taking over a job that I was not equipped to do. Our flesh was never built to be selfdependent. We were created to depend on our Creator, walking in step with the Spirit (Galatians 5:25-26). Our flesh is incapable of pleasing God on its own, but it's OK because we don't have to do it on our own.

The Holy Spirit is always ready to lead us. However, I am convinced that a good portion of believers are not cashing in on the gift that is the Holy Spirit. Maybe it's because of a very religious upbringing that made you afraid of even the thought of the Holy Spirit. It could be disbelief plaguing you. It could be that you just aren't sure of what it means to have a relationship with the Holy Spirit. Maybe you have been a little distant from the Lord or maybe you just have been in a spiritually dry place. Don't allow these things to keep you from unwrapping this gift. Pray that God will release you from the bondage that has kept you from experiencing the fullness of your God relationship. This is critical in taking the next step in our journey.

Study Verse - Galatians 5:22-23

"But the fruit of the Spirit is love, joy, peace, patience, kindness, goodness, faithfulness, gentleness, self-control; against such things there is no law." Galatians 5:22-23 NASB

" But the Holy Spirit produces this kind of fruit in our lives: love, joy, peace, patience, kindness, goodness, gentleness, self-control. There is no law against these things!" Galatians 5:22-23 NIV

The Holy Spirit is the cultivator of spiritual fruit in our lives, including joy. Without that vital relationship, it is impossible to experience Christ's lasting joy because we will remain detached from the source. Being intentional about engaging with the Holy Spirit and surrendering our flesh to the authority of Christ prepares the soil of our heart for the Spirit to plant and cultivate His fruit. The fruit that we are all meant to partake in.

Discovery #5- Why Am I Here?

Ah, the age old question. This is undoubtedly one of the most asked questions, that we ask ourselves other than "What should I wear today?" or "What should I eat?" This question is great because living in our purpose can be vital to our level of happiness. Knowing what God has put you on this earth to do is priceless. Most of the world is so busy trying to find its purpose that they are getting lost in the process and aren't really figuring anything out, which is sad. Even sadder though, is that hardly anyone is looking in the right place, the word of God.

The question "Why am I here?" really can set the mind on an endless path. Unfortunately, many times when we ask ourselves this question, we are not realistic with our expectations for the answer. Instead of really trying to figure out why we are here or what our true gifts are, we may be focused on what looks good and possibly say to ourselves, "That looks good, maybe I'll try that." Most times this kind of thinking leads to a broken heart or to a place that God did not have in the will for your life. Though there is nothing wrong with having big dreams, we have to honestly evaluate the validity of those dreams. Also, we have to recognize the difference between living in our will and God's will for us as well as taking an honest look at the gifts entrusted to us. If you are tone deaf, your dreams of being a solo artist are probably not going to be realized. In the same token, just because you have a beautiful voice doesn't mean that becoming a huge rock star is a part of God's plan for your life.

The truth of the matter is....we all have the same overall purpose in this life here on earth and that is to bring God glory. But if we want to look a little deeper, there are two major categories: #1- Love God #2 – Love people.

"And he said to him 'You shall love the Lord your God with all your heart and with all your soul and with all your mind. This is the great and first commandment. And a second is like it: You shall love your neighbor as yourself. On these two commandments depend all the Law and the Prophets."
Matthew 22:31-40

Our purpose is pretty clear. And how we live out that purpose in our own lives generally relies on the gifts that we have been given (also, our proximity, capacity and willingness). We have all been adorned with gifts that are useful for bringing glory to the Father and the building of the Kingdom of God. We are all responsible for the use of those gifts. *"In his grace, God has given* us *different gifts .....* " *Romans 12:6 NLT.* We are not responsible for coming up with a talent/gift, it's already present. We are only responsible for submitting it to the Lord and using the talent/gift that we have been given for His glory and not our own. Scripture makes clear our reason for being here with passages that point to God's purposes for us and how He intends to fulfill His purposes. Our diligent study of Scripture weeds out confusion and plants seeds of wisdom and purpose.

Highlighted within Biblical text we also find the gifts we receive from the Holy Spirit. *"A spiritual gift is given to each of us so we can help each other."* 1 Corinthians 12:7 NLT. These gifts are equally important to our other gifts. These gifts allow us to operate through the Spirit. Gifts like discernment, great faith, miracles, and others (1Cor. 12:8-11). Spiritual gifts are a great source of edification, encouragement and direction for God's people. Our natural gifts and our spiritual gifts, coupled together with obedience, form the individual part of a broader picture. Our purpose in life collectively is to be disciples for Christ and we are equipped to do so in different ways. Searching for a purpose outside of God's will can only lead down a wide path to destruction that will most times lead you back to the same question, "Why am I here?"

Get into the Word, search yourself and pray frequently about God's will for your life. Once our will lines up with God's will we can really see the Father's purposes come to life in us. I encourage you to actively use your God given gifts so that you can bless and be blessed. Your gifts were given to you so that you could give of them for His glory.

Study Verse- Romans 12:6-8, 13 NLT

6"In his grace, God has given us different gifts for doing certain things well. So if God has given you the ability to prophesy, speak out with as much faith as God has given you. If your gift is serving others, serve them well. If you are a teacher, teach well. If your gift is to encourage others, be encouraging. If it is giving, give generously. If God has given you leadership ability, take the responsibility seriously. And if you have a gift for showing kindness to others, do it gladly."

13"When God's people are in need, be ready to help them. Always be eager to practice hospitality."

Discovery #6- Fix Your Eyes

Letting our happiness depend on our circumstance, is a natural flesh tendency. Its like clock work for us to take the equation of circumstance and outcome to come up with a seemingly logical conclusive emotion. This goes all the way back to Eve in the Garden of Eden. In her logic, it made perfect sense that if she wanted more out of the abundant life she already had, she would have to make the choice to eat of the fruit so she could have knowledge and then she would be satisfied (Genesis 1).

However, we know that that story did not end in satisfaction. The story ended in shame and regret.

Our poor sister Eve thought changing her circumstance was what she needed to do to be satisfied. This is the lie we believe today, all too often. We mistakenly give a job to something or someone that never signed up for employment. We get married believing that our spouse will make us happy, we have children with thinking that parenthood will bring us joy, we seek out things that we believe will bring us happiness, we look for the perfect house because we will finally be happy there, we chase money thinking that financial security will satisfy us.

These lies have left us in constant wonder. None of the things we have searched out in pursuit of happiness could ever produce the joy that our souls pant for. Giving these things the job of bringing joy is giving responsibility to a very unqualified source. A spouse is for companionship, children are for loving and rearing, things are for pleasure, houses are for shelter, and money is for provision. We have to evaluate our expectations and detach our dependence from the tangible and attach it to the ever-faithful Father.

In our daily lives, it can be really easy to focus on all the chaos happening around us and want for different circumstances that might give us solace and satisfaction; the bills that are due and the lack of money to pay them, a struggling marriage, wayward children or ill family members, failing friendships. The noise of this life can have such a stentorian impact and be so distracting. The constant pounding from our surroundings wearing down the barriers that we have put between us and the enemy. There is always something and just because we are children of God, we are not exempt from the trials and tribulations of this world. We have actually already been pre-warned (1Peter 4:12-13 NLT). There is a bit of comfort though, because the hard times we endure in this life will earn us eternal glory. *"For our light and momentary troubles are achieving for us an eternal glory that far outweighs them all."* 2 Corinthians 4:17 NIV.

It's crucial to have an eternal view in order to see our earthly lives from the proper perspective. *"So we fix our eyes not on what is seen, but on what is unseen, since what is seen is temporary, but what is unseen is eternal."* 2 Corinthians 4:18 NIV. A vapor is all we have on this planet (James 4:14 NKJV). Our lives here are simply fog breathed from the Father's mouth for a limited existence. We have to be present in that allotted time making the most of our time. Realizing that we are only living in a temporary circumstance gives us proper perspective and the hope we need to weather life's storms and focus on what is truly important. God's will for our lives. It's so much easier to have joy when you have a clear vision of truth and can see through the lies and trials to the reward. Our trials are the race and eternity with Jesus is the eternal reward. That being said, just like every race, the participants have to make a conscience choice to run and go the distance in order to receive the prize.

So the next time you are surrounded by want, trouble, and expectation, remember to fix your eyes elsewhere. Chose to run the race in the lane that God has designed specifically for you and find your joy in the things unseen knowing where your hope lies.

Study Verse - Job 11:16 NIV

"You will surely forget your trouble, recalling it only as waters gone by."

Discovery #7- Conforming or Conquering?

Our world can seem so frightening and inviting all at the same time. There is a force that pulls people in to enjoy the things that the world has to offer. That force is called, the devil. He knows all the tricks and traps to put in place that will make people head toward all the wrong things. The devil is the best trickster of them all. The enemy is the king of lies, deception, false imagery, and schemes and the earth is his playground. He knows what people like, what they don't like, what they like to hear and what drives them away. He is well aware of what you like and how you like it served. This is why we now live in a feel good society where many people are convinced that, "if it feels good, then do it" is the right way to be. Humans are quickly being desensitized by a host of sinful lures going on in our world. This generation is convinced that anything goes, which has fed the cyclone the enemy has set up where more and more is being accepted rather than corrected. So now, instead of asking ourselves "Why?" we ask ourselves "Why not?"

The bible makes it very clear that we are not to be of this world. We are supposed to be conquers and not conformers to this world. *"Do not conform any longer to the pattern of this world, but be transformed by the renewing of your mind. Then you will be able to test and approve what God's will is-his good, pleasing and perfect will. "* Romans 12:2 NIVUK. In order for us to be conquers, we have to be prepared to get dressed in the armor of God (Ephesians 6) every day and fight for the salvation of this world. Not become active players of the world around us, assisting the enemy in his ploy against mankind and all of Heaven. We can only play for one team. Besides, we are called to be holy and set apart and we can't be set apart from what we are trying to be a part of.

Once we are reborn in Christ, we are made new in Christ Jesus and not of the flesh. Our flesh dies in that rebirth. Paul writes that he died daily (1 Corinthians 15:31 AMP). Though we were born into this world, we are aliens here. We remain here to complete the mission, to conquer the world for Christ. As Christians we already have the victory over the world through the cross. *"This is love for God: to obey his commands. And his commands are not burdensome, for everyone born of God overcomes the world. This is the victory that has overcome the world, even our faith."* 1 John 5:3-4 NIV. The cross is victory over everything that comes against

God's people (i.e., depression, sickness, temptation, addiction, and so much more) and it will continue to deliver people until the second coming. Picking up your cross daily will remind you that you are set apart and help you to battle the pull to conform to the world.

Yes, I know! It's easier said than done. I can sense that almost every brain reading this will quickly come up with an excuse for why this seems so hard to maintain. Or, how the life we have been given is just so hard to manage in the world we've been given. Or, how your situation is so much different than everyone else's. I totally see how things can be completely mentally consuming and overwhelming and even seem impossible to navigate through. Especially with media, friends and acquaintances around us who seem to be living it up. But never forget, *"I can do all things through Christ who strengthens me."* Philippians 4:13 NKJV. And all things means even the situations that seem impossible. All things means....*ALL THINGS!* We can press on and endure all things because the strength we get is not our own but the strength of Christ that gives us the ability to withstand, persevere, and develop in the midst.

We were made to be so much more and the time is now for us to take up our cross and conquer this world. *"You are the light of the world. A city that is set on a hill cannot be hidden. Nor do they light a lamp and put it under a basket, but on a lamp stand, and it gives light to all who are in the house. Let your light so shine before men, that they may see your good works and glorify your Father in heaven."* Matthew 5:14-16 KJV. Take your place as sons and daughters of the King. Our Father puts us high on a pedestal. Why do we choose to step down and live a life that is not fitting for our royal status? I think it's time to reevaluate where we are and how bright we are allowing our lights to shine. Our relationship with the Lord ignites our light but the world can help you put it out if you let it. Let's conquer this world!

Study Verse - 1 John 4:4 NKJV

"You are of God, little children, and have overcome them, because He who is in you is greater than he who is in the world."

Discovery #8- The Enemy

Our human nature has a tendency to get us into a lot of trouble. We let our flesh take over sometimes and go down the wrong path and then just expect to have grace given to us. Though God so freely gives us grace without our pleading, for some reason, it is like pulling teeth for us to give grace to our fellow man.

Sometimes we just can't look past what we see or feel in order to just love like God loves. Circumstance can cause us to get caught up in the assumption that some people are our enemy because of certain confrontations or happenings.

The truth is that we only have one true enemy.....Satan. He is the one who offers opportunity for evil to prevail. He corrupts, lies, steals, kills and devours. Causing havoc among us and ripping joy from our clutches if we allow him to. Key word, *ALLOW*. Droves of us have made the mistake of giving the enemy more power than he actually has and far more credit than he deserves. Our natural reaction can lean towards the "woe is me" type of attitude and help us to play the victim. Not to say that we are not under attack, but we have far more of an upper hand than we realize. We forget that the enemy only has the space that we give him. It's just like that old saying, "Give him a foot and he'll take a mile". That's exactly what he does. The enemy can only use what you give him to use.

Our sinful nature is constantly at war with our spirit man, and ultimately it is our choice of how we want to respond to the spiritual battle inside and to the offers of the enemy. We make the choices to make those sinful thoughts a reality even though Satan uses our sinful nature to tempt and prod us into sinful acts. *"Be alert and of sober mind. Your enemy the devil prowls around like a roaring lion looking for someone to devour." 1 Peter 5:8 NIV*. But that's ok, because there is a redeemer who lives to give us strength to overcome and unspeakable joy. Jesus is the victor over the true enemy.

The people we consider our enemies, are simply people who need to be loved with the love of the God just like us. They need grace, mercy, love, peace just like the rest of us. All of the energy we spend going against each other, fighting with each other or harboring un-forgiveness should really be directed toward spiritual warfare. The warfare we need to wage is against the true enemy because he is the source of evil. Accepting the battle as a flesh-to-flesh battle is counterproductive and disobedient. The way we chose to deal with the evil directed toward us ultimately tells us how far we have come in our spiritual walk. Giving in to what the enemy has directed at us by returning evil for evil is exactly the opposite of what the Lord has directed us to do. *"Resist him, standing firm in the faith, because you know that the family of believers throughout the world is undergoing the same kind of sufferings."* 1 Peter 5:9 NIV.

The stress of focusing on those who are against us drains us of the joy that comes from the One who is for us. That is exactly what the true enemy wants. Relieve yourself of the burden of negative relationships, negative feelings and judgment toward others. Instead, care for your foes, *"If your enemy is hungry, give him food to eat; if he is thirsty, give him water to drink." Proverbs 25:21 NIV.* If we give love and mercy to the people who seem like our enemies, God receives the glory, Satan is defeated and we are blessed.

Study Verse - John 15:17 NIV

"This is my command: Love each other"

Discovery #9-Falsehood

Growing up we dream and imagine all kinds of things that take us to other worlds and allow us to be all sorts of characters. Most little girls want to be a princess or a bride or from time to time a dinosaur. Boys generally opt for more painful characters like wrestlers, robots, and the occasional living room acrobat. Bringing pain to all resting furniture. What a joy it is to live in a world of "no worries," where you can make up all your surroundings and react to make believe situations. Wouldn't it be great if we could walk this out in adulthood? We could just pretend that the bills were paid and never get a disconnect notice. Or dream that the house was clean and waa-laa, carpet stains gone and laundry done! Who are we kidding? There is nothing realistic about that.

As ridiculous as it sounds for us to make believe our realities and live by the delusion that we've conjured up, we make the choice to live this way when we live and make choices in reflection of the lies that we believe. The lies we believe and misconceptions we have set a tone for the way we live and react.

The many discoveries and revelations we make over the course of our journey together will mean nothing if we still hang on to the lies that we have believed over the course of our existence.

We are bombarded with lies from the moment we breathe fresh air. Everything surrounding us produces images for us to store and experiences for us to build on. Our walk through life is an extended screenplay that is in constant edit mode. All that we are exposed to changes the script little by little. Every lie we take on as a truth takes us further down the path of deception and further away from the truths that forms stability. Living a life based on falsehoods that have been built up create false realities, false perceptions, false hopes, and unrealistic expectations. I am choosing to address this issue early on because we must combat the lies of the enemy in order to navigate our way through God's truth to discover and unwrap the gifts that we have been given. The enemy would like nothing more than for us to be in a cloud of deceit. Take in this truth about our enemy.

"…………He was a murderer from the beginning, and does not stand in the truth, because there is no truth in him. When he lies, he speaks out of his own character, for he is a liar and the father of lies."
John 8:44 ESV

We have believed so many lies in our lifetime that many times it can be hard to recognize the truth. It's as if we are trying to swing through the jungle on what we think are vines and then when it's too late, we realize they were actually snakes hanging from the trees. Before we know it, we're bit. That's the trouble with deception. It could very well look like the truth, while offering very different outcomes. But, if you look close enough, you can see the eyes on the snake. Seeking God's truth helps us to recognize the snakes that hang from the trees so that we can swing from the secure vine that won't turn around and bite us. The true Vine, Jesus.

"I am the vine; you are the branches. Whoever abides in me and I in him, he it is that bears much fruit, for apart from me you can do nothing." John 15:1-5 ESV

Our happiness cannot be based on a falsehood. Neither can our joy be produced out of a created ideal that has sprouted from disillusion and deception. Our realities are only beneficial to us when they are built on truth and the Author of that truth. We must expose and dispose of the lies and replace them with God's fortifying freeing actualities that He so graciously gifts us.

Discovery #10-Only When

Christmas is our family's favorite time of year. We love everything about it. We usually unleash every holiday tradition we can find and even some made up ones just to fill in the calendar. The kids love all the fun stuff but they really enjoy taking advantage of all the sugary goodness that comes along with the season. We plan out several "all hands on deck" type of events that keep us really busy but it's always really clear what the kids are looking forward to during the whole count down. Christmas Day. I'm sure, like when I was a kid, they have the whole Christmas morning played out in their minds the day after Thanksgiving. Then when Christmas comes, you can see in their little twinkling eyes that all they can think about is what's under the wrapping paper. And, after we pray and begin the process of handing out the gifts, you can see the relief on their faces and pure glee. Though they are no doubt very grateful to us as we hand them gifts, their minds are completely consumed by the gift and the giver is just kind of a means to an end.

Is this how we treat our Gift Giver?

Have we reduced Him to a means to an end?

These are hard questions to consider and they may burn a little but this may be true for some of us. Some of us may be seeking the gift and not the Gift Giver, looking for fulfillment in what we receive. It was never the plan for us to be satisfied by the blessing. We have been created to be satisfied by the God who put the desires in us. Though God is our ultimate provider no matter what, we must first recognize and honor Him as Lord and Giver. When we reduce Him to a resource, we make the grave mistake of missing out on the incomparable relational value that comes with knowing the Father and walking with the Son. We also shift our worship from the Creator to the created.

In all of our research and discovering, there is one truth that we need to hold tightly. No matter how we dice this thing up. The only way we can experience Christ's lasting joy is to choose Christ's lasting word and ways. His ways will make a way for us. *"Blessed is everyone who fears the Lord , who walks in his ways! You shall eat the fruit of the labor of your hands; you shall be blessed, and it shall be well with you."* Psalm 128:1-2 ESV. We must seek the Giver before the gift.

"When a man's ways please the Lord , he makes even his enemies to be at peace with him. Better is a little with righteousness than great revenues with injustice. The heart of man plans his way, but the Lord establishes his steps." Proverbs 16:7-9 ESV

Pins of Truth

I know we have uncovered quite a bit in this early part of this journey. And, I know that it can be hard to deal with all that is being revealed and attempt to keep the truth of Scripture in view. Trust me, we are all in the same boat. Here's what I propose we do about it. A while back I wanted to give a group of ladies I was speaking to a way to place God's Word in every possible location so that they could always have it in their view. Post-its are great but they lose their stickiness after a while and you can't move them all over the place. I wrecked my brain about it, and then asked God for a solution. The solution.......clothespins! So simple and yet genius! You can write on them and move them wherever you like.

Ever since, I have placed clothespins with God's truths all over the place. On my purse, sitting on my window sill, in my laundry room, on my vanity, pinned to the side of mirrors, in the car, you name it. I now call these, "pins of truth".

Today I want you to go out and get you a pack of clothes pins (usually a little over a dollar). Together we will write words of the Father on them and place these pins of truth right at eye level so that our eyes will be flooded with His truth constantly. The enemy hates for us to know the truth because the lies he feeds us can't hold up against it. When we are filled with the power that comes from the consumption of Scripture, we can be confident in our defense against the enemy.

If you are on social media, show us how you are pinning truth by taking a photo and tagging it with: #pinsofTruth and #thetruthabouthappinessbook. It will be fun for us to all be encouraged by one another in this way and inspire others to be active seekers of God's truth.

CHOICE CHALLENGE #1:

Making the Choice to Gorge

So here we are at our first choice challenge! These challenges will do just that, CHALLENGE you. I'd say we are at as best a place as any to embark on this challenge. If you have been feeling a little spiritually dried out, disengaged, or just plain off, you are in the right place! If you have been wondering how to get on track with what God wants for you, you're in the right place. Or, if you just simply want to get a fresh word, you're in the right place. This challenge will require us to possibly make a new schedule for ourselves or shift a few things around. More importantly, it will require us to make mindful decisions during the course of our day. This is why it's a challenge, I guess.

Now that we have done a bit of investigating, the timing is perfect for us to get deep into the truth of Scripture where we can combat the lies of the enemy with the inerrant Word of God.

Today we are "Making the Choice to Gorge". Generally, gorging isn't exactly looked at as a positive but in this circumstance it's OK. We're choosing to gorge on God's Word. To never get full and eat all we can, whenever we can. *"People do not live on bread alone but by every word that comes from the mouth of God." Matthew 4:4*. I don't think most people really look at how essential the Word is in our lives until we are dry and wondering what's going on. You know how it is. One minute you're on fire for the Lord, feeling on top of your spiritual game and then "all of a sudden", we feel like we're out on a raft in the middle of the ocean wondering what happened. Feeling lifeless and blank. Not realizing that somewhere in the journey we have been malnourished. Our appetite for God's word had been doused by neglect.

So here we are with these thoughts. But, what now? What if we did a preemptive strike? What if we stayed full? What if we just kept the hunger enticed by feeding it small doses all day long? Well.....that's what we are going to do. We are going to fit the Word of God in at every opening of the day. When it gets quiet, when we walk by our bibles, when we pick up our phones, or any chance we have space to think about it. Because, let's face it, we need it like air, so we might as well breathe it in as often. *"For the word of God is alive and powerful. It is sharper than the two-edged sword, cutting between soul and spirit, between bone and marrow. It exposes our innermost thoughts and desires." Hebrews 4:12.* The Word is life for us. It gives us the power, wisdom and heart we need to be set on fire by the Holy Spirit. We cannot neglect our spirits need for a constant serving of God's Word.

Prayer:

Lord Jesus, thank You for Your Word. You have given me so much provision through Your promises and guidance. Today, God, I ask that You please place a burning desire inside of me to gorge on Your word. Let me never get full. Open my eyes to see every opportunity where I can take a bite of Scripture. May all these things bring You glory. In Jesus Name, AMEN!

May your heart ever hunger for the food of the Spirit!

My Journey

What lies have I believed about happiness/joy?

What areas have I conformed to instead of conquered?

Where have I given the enemy the upper hand in my perspective?

Discussion Questions

What did I learn about myself in this section?

What Scriptures stood out to me in this section?

What life application do I intend to implement with the discoveries that I have made?

Journaling Page

_____

_____

_____

_____

_____

_____

_____

_____

_____

_____

_____

_____

_____

_____

_____

_____

_____

_____

_____

_____

_____

_____

_____

Part 2

It's A Heart Thing

Now that we've made some headway in our journey, let's take a step toward resolving some inner disturbances that stand in between us and our true joy.

The average heart beats 60-100 beats per minute and pumps 2.4 ounces of blood through our veins with every beat. Our hearts are considered the epicenter of our bodies. Our hearts are also the epicenter of our spiritual wellbeing. And, just like our physical hearts pumps blood through our bodies, our spiritual heart pumps elements of truth through us.

The heart tells everything. It spills out our secrets without us ever saying a word. It reveals itself through our actions, our choices, and our mouths. Though we spend many hours trying to cover up what really hides in our hearts, eventually, everything that flows through our hearts is revealed.

Guard Your Heart

Our heart holds the keys to many occurrences in our human response to the circumstances around us. It spills out from our mouths and our hands. Our actions and the things we say are a direct reflection of the condition of our hearts. So, it makes perfect sense to protect that which has so much control. The thought of guarding your heart can appear like a simple external practice. However, many of us don't even recognize that we have left our hearts wide open. I mean, most people don't intentionally open their lives to heartache, trials, suffering, and evil. The majority of humans go through life with the assumption that they are doing the best they can.

We make relationships with people and really don't think past the surface of it or of the spiritual attachments that we are making. We engage sin through all of our senses. In our entertainment and activities, letting the wrong someone get too close or befriending someone who leads a not so holy life and begin to walk the wide path with them. Then, we assume that we are ok because we have a
"relationship" with Christ not realizing that we are still accountable for the actions that we have participated in. We totally miss the mark as we carry on in our blatant disobedience or complacency.

Our unguarded heart allows us to be persuaded and blinded. Leading us to be deaf to the voice of the Spirit, therefore, inviting compromise and conformity. An unguarded heart is a misled heart. As heirs to the

Kingdom of God, The Spirit of God is our guide, but we can't hear the Spirit if we have other voices speaking to our hearts. *"For those who are led by the spirit of God, are the children of God."* Romans 8:14 NIV

So, if we are true children of God and we have given our hearts over to Christ, why are we sometimes so careless with His heart? Why is it easier for us to put a fence around the homes we live in than around the home that Jesus lives in? Maybe it's because we don't have a realistic grasp on what it means for Christ to be alive in us. Truly, I believe that if we could really get the visual of what it looks like for Jesus to be living in our hearts and keep it, we would do a much better job at allowing God to create in us a clean heart and putting up a secure fence around His home.

Keeping boundaries around our hearts/minds is exactly what it takes to prevent temptation from becoming sin. *"Guard your heart above all else, for it determines the course of your life."* Proverbs 4:23 NLT. We must be mindful of the company we keep and the type of influences we give access to our hearts. We have a responsibility to be careful to keep the Lord's home clean and ready to use. Not to say that we should totally cut people or some things off. However we should be mindful if what we are engaging in brings any glory to God as well as if our boundaries are going to be weakened by what we are doing. For example, if you watch a movie with a lot of foul language and then you notice that you have begun to say a curse word here and there, chances are your mind has been infiltrated a bit. You've allowed yourself to receive those words and now you have to try and figure out how to get rid of what you have let in. Now the living room of the Lord's home is a little messy.

Guarding the heart is of the utmost importance because everything that we do is a result of what our heart contains. *"For from the heart come evil thoughts, murder, adultery, all sexual immorality, theft, lying, and slander."* Matthew 15:19 NLT. Protecting your heart is stopping damage before it can wreak havoc on your life. Putting standards in place so that you won't even have to worry about the trouble of being enticed to do wrong is wise and rewarding.

My challenge for all of us: this week, be mindful of our surroundings. Let's rethink our "heart boundaries." Then, let's ask ourselves, "Where is there a gap in the fence of our heart?" This is a challenge that is one of the most important and revealing. Take the time to pray and seek the Lord for discernment and guidance.

No Weapons Shall Prevail

Defeated: having suffered defeat; beaten.

Unfortunately, we humans are bombarded by a variety of joy depleting feelings. The feeling of being defeated and/or discouraged is quite the quick happiness zapper. The feeling usually sets in when we feel like life isn't going in the direction we anticipated. Or, simply when life hands us lemons. I know in my case, I have wallowed in defeat when the chips were down many times. When the walls are caving in around you, it's quite the feat to see the truth of where you stand. Fortunately, for the children of God, there is no defeat for those who trust in Him. Defeat is only a word that exists in your life if you allow it to. Our happiness can only fully take shape when we understand the concept that we always have the victory, because for Christ's followers all things work together for the good (Romans 8:28).

The enemy can only penetrate our barricades of faith if we let him. Our trust and faith in the Lord is our defense against all opposition. *"If anyone does attack you, it will not be my doing; whoever attacks you will surrender to you."* Isaiah 54:15 NIV. With this truth, we should wallow in the joy that we have been given rather than the defeat that was thrown at us.

Our God is the creator of all. *"See, it is I who created the blacksmith who fans the coals into flame and forges a weapon fit for its work. And it is I who have created the destroyer to wreak havoc;"* Isaiah 54:16 NIV. Though it may seem like all the arrows are pointed at you, the truth is that our Lord has already redirected the arrows and we are in the clear. No matter what it looks like, we have the victory. Defeat is only a six-letter word not the judgment upon us.

Only when you receive defeat, are you defeated.

We have access to a heritage of victory transferred to us through Christ Jesus. The Word is our sword of truth against all evil that comes against us and the Lord ensures that even the bad circumstances work in our favor. *"no weapon forged against you will prevail, and you will refute every tongue that accuses you. This is the heritage of the servants of the Lord, and this is their vindication from me," declares the Lord."* Isaiah 54:17 NIV. Our lemons are always made into lemonade. Though it can seem like we are just holding lots of lemons, the Lord holds the pitcher (us) ready for the making. Every trial is a lemon being squeezed adding more juice to your pitcher and, when you've gone through all your lemons, God stirs it all up, adds sugar (rewards) and we get our lemonade, us in the will of God.

Study Verse- Isaiah 54:10, 17 NIV

10 "Though the mountains be shaken and the hills be removed, yet my unfailing love for you will not be shaken nor my covenant of peace be removed," says the Lord, who has compassion on you. "

17 "no weapon forged against you will prevail, and you will refute every tongue that accuses you. This is the heritage of the servants of the Lord, and this is their vindication from me," declares the Lord." **Finding Refuge in Him**

In the past, I have been a victim of anxiety. Anyone who has ever dealt with anxiety can totally relate when I say that it brings some of the most out of control emotional and physical symptoms. You almost feel trapped in your own body while all of your insides are trying to escape. Even worse, you feel like everyone thinks you're crazy and you kind of feel that way. In an instant, it can make you feel totally alone in a room full of people.

You know how it is when you are going through something and you feel like there is no one around to talk to. You feel totally alone in the situation, like no one understands or cares how you feel. This feeling of isolation and bondage is a horrible place to be. Making us feel completely out of control. These situations make us vulnerable, causing a haze to come between our common sense and our situation. In these moments our feelings can cause us to make hasty decisions in the wrong direction and lead us to rely on human survival instinct. We get panicked and run to the nearest human who seems like they can help us. We get some great advice (hopefully) and then try to figure out what we can do to solve our dilemma. All this, for us to still be worked up by the end of it all and often more confused than before we started.

Fortunately for us, there is someone who is just waiting for us to come running to Him looking for comfort and refuge. His name is…. God! He is always there, even when we feel alone. *"I know the Lord is always with me. I will not be shaken, for he is right beside me."* Psalm 16:8 NLT. He knows what we are going through and how we feel. The Lord has been through every hardship. He has been hungry, betrayed, beaten, laughed at, abandoned, you name it. He has been through it all and has overcome it all. Even on our behalf.

Not only is He with us all the time but He protects us as well. If we let Him, we can avoid a lot of harm. *"You are my refuge and my shield; your word is my source of hope."* Psalm 119:114 NLT. The last thing I'm sure He wants to see is His children suffering when He is trying so hard to keep them from the devil's grasp. The enemy is doing everything in his power to keep us from the safety of God's umbrella. The devil gets into your head and tells you everything you do or don't want to hear to draw you away. When you are going through a rough patch is when you are most vulnerable but those are the times when you need to cling tight to the Lord and the Word. You will find strength in both because even though the surroundings don't look so good, God is using this time to build you up and prepare you for what He has called you for while the enemy is doing His best to make you feel alone and forgotten.

Joy lies in the one who gives it. Our heavenly Father. There is no refuge in this world for those of us who are not of this world. Stop looking around you and start looking above for your help. *"We wait in hope for the Lord; he is our help and our shield."* Psalm 33:20 NIV.

Study Verse- Psalm 34:8 NLT

"Taste and see that the Lord is good. Oh, the joys of those who take refuge in him!"

Time With Your Father

Wading through the waters of life, can occasionally feel like you're fighting for your life in an alligator filled Louisiana swamp. You feel like you are just barely surviving and there is no time for anything else but looking ahead to achieve the next task. We get into our "schedules" and make our own "plans," and figure as long as we can get to evening time we have done it and then it starts all over again the next day.

With the lives that most of us lead, it can seem hard to find time to take a breath let alone make time to sit in quiet and have a good time of prayer. However, as impossible as it seems, it is a good contributor to lasting joy. Not to mention the most important factor, a healthy relationship with your Savior, Father, and Friend. After all, we could all use a good friend to talk to who won't repeat what we have said to someone else, or remind us of what we have done in the past. What better friend than Jesus? He already knows everything about us. Even the things that we have never told a soul and He still wants us. Not to mention that He has the solutions to our problems. He's pretty much the best friend you ever have, if you allow Him to come in and be that for you. The tithe of your time blesses the remainder of your time. Your days are easier to deal with and you will find that God's peace rest in you more noticeably.

The Lord is just waiting for us to turn and face Him to commune with Him. It is one of His greatest joys. *"The Lord detests the sacrifice of the wicked, but he delights in the prayers of the upright."* Proverbs 15:8

NLT. He loves for His children to run into His arms and tell Him all about how they feel or what they want, or need. And just as much as He enjoys hearing our prayers, He enjoys answering them, *"Keep on asking, and you will receive what you ask for. Keep on seeking, and you will find. Keep on knocking, and the door will be opened to you."* Matthew 7:7 NLT. Not to mention that He holds all the treasures of the world and heaven in His hands. He wants to bless us and He wants us to give us His joy. *"So if you sinful people know how to give good gifts to your children, how much more will your heavenly Father give good gifts to those who ask him."* Matthew 7:11 NLT. What more could you want in a friend? I'm pretty sure that none of our friends listed on social media can do any of these things for us.

Our prayer time is an escape from the world around us as we enter into the throne room of Christ. We have the full attention of the God of the universe. Coming into His courts and laying our burdens at His feet brings freedom and peace. You can go straight to the Father and lay all your worries at His feet and leave them there for Him to take care of. When you lay them down and don't pick them back up. Once you have prayed about something, leave it alone. If you are going to still worry about it, you might as well not pray about it because your worry says that you don't have faith that God is going to take care of it. Just as you don't take your money to the bank teller and then turn around and leave with the same money you came in with. You make a deposit and walk out. That is exactly what you should do with your burdens. Take it to God in prayer and deposit it, then walk away from it.

Our intimate dialogue with God is very important. Equally important is learning to just sit in His presence and listen for His voice. Inviting Him into your space and then just sitting with Him without saying a word. This creates a welcoming space for His Spirit to enter in undisturbed.

Here's a challenge. Keep a prayer journal. Write what you pray about every day. When you pray, Praise Him for the greatness of who He is and thank the Lord for what He has done for you. Then, you pray for others and for yourself. Always be thankful in your prayers! He has already done so much for us. When you receive the answer to your prayer, whether it's the answer you want or not, write it down. This will get you in the practice of making prayer time a habit. Remember, what may seem like a no answer is still an answer. Sometimes we think we are not getting what we asked for, when He may be saying, "I have something better," or "not right now." He loves you and will protect you if something you want may not be good for you or the will He has for your life in the grand scheme of things. He's a good Father!

Study Verse - Colossians 4:2 NLT

"Devote yourselves to prayer with an alert mind and a thankful heart."

CHOICE CHALLENGE #2:

Making the Choice to BE

Hopefully you have been able to take something from the first of our choice challenges and put it into practice. I must say that these challenges will be easier to read than to execute on a consistent basis. So, if you feel like you are the only one having to remind yourself of the challenges all the time, you are not alone! Thank God for grace! Just a suggestion, maybe we should write these down on a post-it and put it on the back of our phones or write it on our hands as a closer reminder. Either way, it's time for our next challenge so let's jump right in feet first!

Walking around my humble abode and assessing my work load for the day can be a bit daunting every morning. I literally say to myself sometimes, "I feel like the walls are closing in on me," when I'm in my life stricken closet. I stand there wondering how in the world things can be so messy when all I do is clean and rearrange all day long. Are there little mean elves that come out every night and multiply my workload? I mean seriously, the only time I get to sit is when I'm writing and when the sun goes down and sometimes on its way up again. But maybe that's the problem. Maybe I'm not taking the time to just BE. The time to just be alive in the mess. To just be present and not busy with all the doing.

So today, we are "Making the Choice to BE". And by <u>BE</u> I mean to "**B**e Still & **E**ngaged." We can be so busy that we forget who is in control of it all and by default become detached from our place of refuge and strength. *"Be still and know that I am God….."* Psalm 46:10. We tend to forget that we can find rest, protection and assurance there. It's about knowing and trusting. Trusting that our Father is already making provision and has a bigger plan than what we can see. Knowing that we can trust that He is who He says He is.

If we just slow down and be still we will start to see that, no, the walls are not closing in on us and there aren't little mean elves trying to secretly give us a nervous break down. We will see that our busyness and mental chaos has caused us to get caught up in the doing and we have forgotten to KNOW that He is God. All the shuffling around can easily get our Holy Spirit lifeline tangled and disengaged. This domino effect can get way out of hand if we don't wrangle it in at the start.

On this bright and hopeful day, we are going to STOP all the bustle and shuffle. Take a couple deep breaths as we actively still our hearts and get engaged with the Holy Spirit. This challenge is going to take lots of prayer and intentional action on our behalf. The sweeping can wait, the call can wait, the kid can wait and the media can wait, so that we can plug back into the source of life. *"All praise to God, the Father of our Lord Jesus Christ. God is our merciful Father and the source of all comfort. He comforts us in all our troubles, so that we can comfort others. When they are troubled, we will be able to give them the same comfort God has given us.* " 2 Corinthians 1:3-4 NLT **Prayer**:

Lord Jesus, thank You for Your unfailing grace that covers me in the busy times. God, today I surrender my doing to You. Give me the strength to BE today. Help me to be okay with being still and intentional about being engaged with Your Spirit. I bind every distraction that would hinder me from connecting with Your will for me today. In Jesus Name, Amen!!

My Journey

What area in my life have I neglected to guard my heart?

What adjustments do I need to make in my daily life to do a better job at protecting my heart?

Where have I searched for refuge other than the Father?

What can I do to ensure time with the Father on a consistent and meaningful basis?

Discussion Questions

What did I learn about myself in this section?

What Scriptures stood out to me in this section?

What life application do I intend to implement with the discoveries that I have made?

Journaling Page

Part 3

Learning the Art
of the Release

Put Your Eggs in His Basket

As a kid, one of the holidays I remember enjoying the most was Easter. Not necessarily for the reasons we celebrate, but for all the goodies (of course) that came with the holiday. The excitement and the build up to the day created a giddy atmosphere in my little world. Then, on Easter Day, when I would put my lace gloved hands on that pretty basket, I would light up at the thought of all the eggs I would find and put in my new basket. I remember when we would hunt for eggs in the yard, if I dropped one, I would frantically turn around and quickly pick it up, afraid that another kid would get it. Never mind the fact that I would get treats no matter what. I spent so much time trying not to drop the eggs that it was hard to run because I was so concentrated on the basket.

This tactic of recovery may have snuck its way into adulthood. We get so wrapped up in collecting the eggs of life and trying to keep them in our baskets that we have a hard time running.

Maybe all of us must have some deep desire to be in a circus or something. We try the balancing act of trying to keep everything just right. We try being clowns, with our painted on faces, so that everyone will think that things are "fine." We try taming the lions, trying to keep our fears and anxieties at bay, so that we can function. Finally, we attempt the most difficult one. We try to juggle eggs in a basket without breaking them. Each egg represents hundreds of thoughts and tasks. We have our organizers and calendars full of things we want to do or think that we need to do. All the while our brains are on the verge of exploding from all of the information we have stuffed into it. This is so exhausting.

Trying to control the uncontrollable is a complete waste of time, and yet we find a reason to think we are capable of doing just that. What is the point of trying to make an immovable plan for our lives when our Father has already put a plan in place? He knows our hearts desires, our wishes, our dreams, and what's best for us so why don't we just let Him take control? I'll tell you why. Our flesh is at constant odds with the will of the Father. Thus, we have to make a conscious effort to surrender our flesh. Our flesh wants to make every decision and count every egg, even when we have yet to realize that the eggs we're so busy counting are breaking because we're holding on so tight. We want to cook the eggs, serve the eggs, and eat the eggs. Leaving nothing for the Father to help us with.

"For we are God's masterpiece. He has created us anew in Christ Jesus, so we can do the good things he planned for us long ago." Ephesians 2:10 NLT.

Anything that He has planned for our lives is much better than any plan we could come up with. He loves us and has everything that we need in His basket. The Father has planned our paths with careful consideration.

As much as we fight against our intended path, God will continue to put our life in order to direct us back onto the right track. This is why sometimes when we make plans or desire something that we don't need in our life, it doesn't work out. For example, if you are in a relationship (any relationship) that does not line up with God's will, the relationship will likely remain in turmoil or be uneasy. This is especially true if the relationship is not a pure one. *"We can make our plans, but the Lord determines our steps."* Proverbs 16:9 NLT. Continuing to try and force something that the Lord does not intend to be a part of our lives will only cause, stress, frustration, depression and heartache. Trusting God as Lord is a great factor in living out the abundant joyful life we're after. Living life without trusting God is like walking through a minefield with a blindfold on. Not very wise at all! *"Trust in the Lord and do good. Then you will live safely in the land and prosper."* Psalm 37:3 NLT.

I don't know about you, but I think that I will keep all of my eggs in His basket and let Him worry about the counting. I challenge you to pray and seek God's will for your life, truly trusting in Him and keeping faith in Him, knowing that He will deliver and make good on His promises to you. Trust Him! He will lead you where you're meant to go, even if it seems like you're not going in that direction. Just stand on your Father the Rock and you will see your desires change and He will give you the desires of your heart. Trust Him, and you will be at peace. Trust Him so that you don't have to worry about where your life is going. Trust Him and experience favor beyond measure. Trust Him and He will give you new life and life abundantly!

Study Verse - Proverbs 16:20 NLT

"Those who listen to instruction will prosper; those who trust the Lord will be joyful."

God Can't Fill a Cup That Is Already Full

Our world is in a constant seeking mode. We are always looking for the next blessing, the next season, the next upgrade, the next job, the next anything. Praying and hoping for something. Then when we don't see things going how we thought they would go, we get a little upset or frustrated. We never really stop to think, "Have I made room for a true blessing in my life?" or "Am I ready to receive what I'm asking for?" or better yet, "What am I doing with what I've already been given?" How can God truly bless us when the space is already full of junk? Or, if we simply have not used what He has already given us, making room for more. Maybe it's our move. Maybe He's waiting for us.

We sometimes eliminate ourselves from this process. It can be easy to slip into the thinking that we should just get what we want no matter if we are prepared for it or not. We can slip into tunnel vision and only see what we desire and nothing else. (Side note: be careful with this. It can be easy to also slip into idolatry with this kind of want.). However, we must give our Father more credit than this. He considers all things and makes good and just decisions. His timing is always perfect and so is His alignment. While we may "feel" ready for something, there may be a vast space between us and ready.

Let's address wrongful placeholders that may be keeping us in a premature state. *"Remove the impurities from silver, and the sterling will be ready for the silversmith."* Proverbs 25:4 NLT. God is the silversmith and we are the silver. We have to let go of things so that we can be ready for the silversmith to work in us.

It can be frightening to let go of those old broken down things that you are holding onto because they remind you of your great aunt Sue, or keeping bad habits because you have been doing them for so long that it feels like a cozy sweater. Honestly think about the junk you're holding onto. Is it beneficial to your life? What value does it hold? The tougher question, are you willing to miss out on what God has for you just to hang onto it? Or are you ready to sacrifice it for the improvement of your life and relationship with Christ? Our hope and security is found in Jesus.

If the spaces in our lives are filled with artificial satisfiers, we will never have room for the authentic satisfaction that comes from the Father. Our fulfillment can only be found in Him. We must know in our heart of hearts that He will take care of us and we don't need anything other than Him to survive this life and be satisfied. *"Look at the birds. They don't plant or harvest or store food in barns, for your heavenly Father feeds them. And aren't you far more valuable to him than they are? Can all your worries add a single moment to your life? And if God cares so wonderfully for wildflowers that are here today and thrown into the fire tomorrow, he will certainly care for you. Why do you have so little faith?"* Matthew 6:26-27, 30 NLT.

We are lovingly considered by the Most High. It's also beneficial to acknowledge the fact that anything we give up for His sake will come back to us plus some. *"And everyone who has given up houses or brothers or sisters or father or mother or children or property, for my sake, will receive a hundred times as much in return and will inherit eternal life."* Matthew 19:29 NLT. Our faith response is met with His generosity and grace. If we truly trust Him, letting go of earthly possessions and bad habits should be easy because we know that we will be rewarded for our sacrifices. Open hands that give are also open to receive. Keep your hands free of junk; it may be taking the place of your blessing.

Now that we've talked about the place takers, let's talk about what He's already put in our cup. How faithful have we been with it? You know the gifts He has already bestowed upon you and the blessings that He has already adorned you with? Maybe, there's talent that no one knows you have or the passion that God has placed in your heart that you keep pushing to the back burner because it's "not the right time." I am totally guilty of this one. I was afraid to let anyone see what gifts I had or what I was capable of. I allowed fear to hold me in a place where I was hoarding the blessings that the Father had given me instead of being a good and grateful steward of the gifts that He gave to me by using them to advance the Kingdom.

Let's take a look into one of Jesus' parables in Matthew 25 that will help us here.

"For it will be like a man going on a journey, who called his servants and entrusted to them his property. To one he gave five talents, to another two, to another one, to each according to his ability. Then he went away. He who had received the five talents went at once and traded with them, and he made five talents more. So also he who had the two talents made two talents more. But he who had received the one talent went and dug in the ground and hid his master's money.

Now after a long time the master of those servants came and settled accounts with them. And he who had received the five talents came forward, bringing five talents more, saying, 'Master, you delivered to me five talents; here I have made five talents more.' His master said to him, 'Well done, good and faithful servant. You have been faithful over a little; I will set you over much. Enter into the joy of your master.' And he also who had the two talents came forward, saying, 'Master, you delivered to me two talents; here I have made two talents more.' His master said to him, 'Well done, good and faithful servant. You have been faithful over a little; I will set you over much. Enter into the joy of your master.' He also who had received the one talent came forward, saying, 'Master, I knew you to be a hard man, reaping where you did not sow, and gathering where you scattered no seed, so I was afraid, and I went and hid your talent in the ground. Here you have what is yours.' But his master answered him, 'You wicked and slothful servant!

You knew that I reap where I have not sown and gather where I scattered no seed? Then you ought to have invested my money with the bankers, and at my coming I should have received what was my own with interest. So take the talent from him and give it to him who has the ten talents. For to everyone who has will more be given, and he will have an abundance. But from the one who has not, even what he has will be taken away. " Matthew 25:14-29 ESV

We beg Him for more, but He has already given us so much that we may not even be using according to His will, or using at all for that matter. It may be due time for us to take inventory of what we already have, sift through and pull out the gems that God has already placed within us. Be courageous, dust off those beauties, shine some light on them, and offer those gifts back to Christ. He will cover them and expand them for His ultimate glory that he so graciously shares with us.

Study Verse- *Mark 4:18-20 NLT*

"The seed that fell among the thorns represents others who hear God's word, but all too quickly the message is crowded out by the worries of this life, the lure of wealth, and the desire for other things, so no fruit is produced. And the seed that fell on good soil represents those who hear and accept God's word and produce a harvest of thirty, sixty, or even a hundred times as much as had been planted!"

Have You Listened To Your Father Today?

One of the hardest things for us as humans to do, especially as adults, is be **<u>OBEDIENT</u>**. Since the beginning of time, the flesh has waged war against righteousness and submission (another dirty word for humans). I have always been a tad bit rebellious in this area in my life journey. Most of us feel like, we are adults and we should be able to do whatever we want to do. However, the issue with that kind of outlook is what we want to do usually gets us in more trouble than our adult selves know how to get out of. Regardless, we will obey something or someone no matter how we feel about obedience. We will either submit to our Father God, Satan, or self. The Lord has put in place guidelines for us to keep us from falling and getting hurt.

Every commandment was formed with the love and protecting heart of the Father who wants to keep His children from heartache. Also, like a good father, He allows us to see the consequences of the choices we make in hopes that we will learn and make a different choice in the future. Like most actions, sin has a cause and effect type of cycle. Unfortunately, or should I say fortunately there are consequences for choosing to disobey the commandments that He has set in place. *"For I command you today to love the Lord your God, to walk in his ways, and to keep his commands, decrees and laws; then you will live and increase, and the Lord your God will bless you in the land you are entering to possess. But if your heart turns away and you are not obedient, and if you are drawn away to bow down to other gods and worship them, I declare to you this day that you will certainly be destroyed. You will not live long in the land you are crossing the Jordan to enter and possess."* Deuteronomy 30:16-18 NIV.

God took hundreds of years putting His book of instruction together for us so that every obstacle in life would be covered. It is our responsibility to be obedient and follow His way towards righteousness. It is also our responsibility to learn from the consequences of disobedience. When we fall and get off track, we need to get up, dust off, and get back on the right path. We should not just say, "Oh well, I've messed up, it doesn't matter what I do now." because the Lord gives us as many chances as there are messups, and that's a lot. All we have to do is repent, turn to Him, and then we have a fresh start.

Listening to God's voice is so important to our growth. He is speaking to us all the time, but many times we can't hear Him because we have either clouded our minds with unnecessary junk or we lead extremely high-octane lives that leave no sound void big enough to get alone with the Lord and hear Him. With five small children, it can be a serious challenge for me to even use the bathroom, let alone trying to find a quiet moment in the day to seek the Lord. It's almost impossible. But I got over feeling like my kids needed me at every moment of the day and started to lock myself away in the bathroom or office or closet on occasion. We need to go to a quiet place, pray and quiet our minds so that we can hear our Father talking to us on a regular basis. Though most times the quiet needs to happen on the outside, we also have to learn the art of emptying the mind in order to quiet our mind enough to hear from the Lord. I mention this because if you're anything like me, your thoughts are probably just as noisy as the world around you. However, if we actively listen to His direction, our lives will be full of peace and joy. He will take you places you never dreamed and bless you with things you never thought you'd have. The Lord is just looking for you to be willing and obedient so that He can bless your socks off. Being obedient to the Word of God brings about righteousness and peace. *"The fruit of righteousness will be peace; the effect of righteousness will be quietness and confidence forever."*
Isaiah 32:17 NIVUK.

Our Father is not trying to keep us from fun or the things we want. He is simply trying to give us a blessed life that will bring Him glory and us peace, joy and abundance. It is in our best interest to obey his instruction and refuse to conform to the ways of the world. We will ultimately have to pay for our rebellion, so why even go in that direction. *"He who scorns instruction will pay for it, but he who respects a command is rewarded."* Proverbs 13:13 NIV. Ask yourself this. Would you rather change your outlook on obedience and be blessed? Or keep doing what you want to do and have a limited life without real joy? Only you can decide.

Study Verse- Ezekiel 33:13 NIVUK

"If I tell the righteous man that he will surely live, but then he trusts in his righteousness and does evil, none of the righteous things he has done will be remembered; he will die for the evil he has done."

A Renewal Of The Mind ....

During coffee with a really great friend of mine, she so eloquently reminded me of something that seems so simple. Something that I have never really had an issue remembering before. Something that had some how become a reoccurring battle in the days surrounding this friendly meeting. She reminded me that, my mindset could limit what God can do for me. It can determine how far I can go in the Lord's will for my life and the spiritual balance in my home, among many other things. What a powerful reminder! Also, kind of a kick in the pants (excuse my French [By the way, that was totally not French]). This was kind of a rebuke for me. A welcomed one though because I am sure that I have reminded her of the same thing at some point or another.

Isn't it great when the wisdom that the Holy Spirit gave you for someone comes back to you? At the time, I'm sure I was completely consumed by my thoughts and didn't realize the tone that was being set for God to do work in me. Let's face it, who really enjoys being told the truth when it burns. I realized that I had been putting a ceiling on God's working space in my life. I had given Him boundaries to the greatness that He could do through me. It was time to snap back to reality, refocus and get a renewed mind.

How quickly we can forget how powerful the thoughts in our mind are and how important it is that we harness them and turn them over to the Father. *"Instead, let the Spirit renew your thoughts and attitudes."* Ephesians 4:23 NLT. We have to learn to relax and let the Holy Spirit guide our mind to new thoughts and our heart towards a new attitude and focus. To renew our mind in Jesus is to renew and refresh our spirit as well. *"That is why we never give up. Though our bodies are dying, our spirits are being renewed every day."* 2 Corinthians 4:16 NLT.

It can be exponentially hard sometimes to look past what we think is supposed to be in order to receive what God says is meant to be. We have to transition to a place where we can get out of our own way and let our minds be transformed, looking upward rather than around us or even in us. *"For our present troubles are small and won't last very long. Yet they produce for us a glory that vastly outweighs them and will last forever!"* 2 Corinthians 4:17 NLT. For what the Lord has for us is far greater than anything we could ever possibly fathom on our own. Our true fruitfulness is a product from heaven not by our own doing.

Therefore I say, be diligent in your journey to be renewed in Jesus. Seek to be renewed in your mind, body and spirit. Let your mind be limitless in what the Lord can do, let your body be His vessel and let your spirit be made new in Jesus every day!

Study Verse - 2 Corinthians 4:18 NLT

"So we don't look at the troubles we can see now; rather, we fix our gaze on things that cannot be seen. For the things we see now will soon be gone, but the things we cannot see will last forever. "

The Non-Given Emotion

One of our biggest intangible problems is **FEAR!** We are afraid of so many different things. We have fear of rejection, fear of success, fear of death, fear of the future and many other things. The definition of

Fear: 1. a. A very unpleasant or disturbing feeling caused by the presence or imminence of danger: *Our fears intensified as the storm approached.* **b.** A state or condition marked by this feeling: *living in constant fear of attack; saved as much as he could for fear of losing his job.* **2.** A feeling of disquiet or apprehension:

a fear of looking foolish. **3.** A reason for dread or apprehension: *Being alone is my greatest fear.*

This feeling is a roadblock for just about everyone, whether admitted or not. Fear is of the devil. It is another one of his lies. Fear is his number one tactic against us. He uses fear to help us justify things that we do or don't do. This one emotion will keep you from reaching your potential in every area of your life. Fear can be compared to trying to walk with concrete shoes on. Attempting to move forward is nearly impossible because of the weight.

Fear weighs you down so that you are incapable of forward motion even causing you to fall backwards from time-to-time. Torturous and paralyzing, fear causes us to see a magnetized version of the negatives. The enemy loves to use this imagery to keep us entangled in fear and doubt. The truth is that our fear is most likely based on false information or imagined scenarios. It creates in us unnecessary defenses and dangerous patterns that cause other chain reactions to occur.

For example, if you have a fear of being let down, there is no way you will be really happy in life. Why? Because there is no way that you will not be let down every now and again. It's a part of life. Fear is the opposite a safe place, it is a very dark place. God has not given us the spirit of fear. He has given us love, joy, peace and power. And more importantly, GRACE! Grace is sufficient enough to get us past any issue. Once we can realize that fear is a lie from the devil, we can begin to move past those barriers that have kept us from becoming the great people that God wants us to be. Giving your fears and worries to Him will alleviate you from the responsibility of trying to win these battles of the mind alone. The battle was won at Calvary. Fear is another unnecessary burden. Today, I challenge you to unload it at the Cross.

Study Verse- 2 Timothy 1:7 NIV

"For the Spirit God gave us does not make us timid, but gives us power, love and self-discipline."

Your Friend, "Worry"

During an extended period of my life, I found myself leaning on my not so friendly friend, "Worry," Even though I am usually the overzealous advocate for thinking positively, for some reason, there have been days that left me feeling a little anxious about things to come. Not being able to plan for my emotional comfort during seasons like these, make me feel a little uneasy. Knowing that these are only seasons does little to calm my frustration and anxiety. Honestly, in the moment, I had just been looking for that particular season to come to a prompt closing. However as I had been getting all worked up in my own head and building different scenarios of how I think things will pan out or should pan out, I began to seek the Word on the subject of worry. Knowing that the Word of God clearly had something better for me.

Now I realize that I had allowed worry to put a small dimmer on the brightness of my joy and contentment. I began thinking of others who are going through the same experience from time-to-time. Worry, is a stealth joy stealer. Very much like its twin brother "Fear", it can build a wedge between us and the Lord with its high non-trust attributes. Mainly because it can start as just being cautious or concerned and then turn into full blown worry and/or anxiety. Turning our focus to the circumstance and not our provider, Christ, hinders our faith and limiting our trust. Worry cancels out trust making it an unprofitable ally. So, what can we do to say good-bye to this unwanted mind invader? It's simple. Let someone else do all the worrying and move forward in trust and faith. *"Casting the whole of your care [all your anxieties, all your worries, all your concerns, once and for all] on Him, for He cares for you affectionately and cares about you faithfully."* 1Peter 5:7.

I know what you're thinking, "easier said than done." It is much easier to get started on the path of trust and freedom than to continue down a road of stress and anxiety toward unhappiness.

Trading in those feelings of frustration and brain bending worry for prayer and seeking the Word of God will build your faith allowing uncertainty to morph into trust. *"Do not fret or have any anxiety about anything, but in every circumstance and in everything, by prayer and petition (definite requests), with thanksgiving, continue to make your wants known to God."* Philippians 4:6 AMP. In those times of frustration, remember how far you have already come and look toward the Father with thanksgiving and you will find the strength to move past your emotions to see through the circumstance to the hope (Romans 5:35). Hope diminishes worry by placing the shield of Faith in front of the circumstance. Helping us to rely on our ever-trustworthy ally, Jesus.

Study Verse- John 14:1

"DO NOT let your hearts be troubled (distressed, agitated). You believe in and adhere to and trust in and rely on God; believe in and adhere to and trust in and rely also on Me."

CHOICE CHALLENGE #3:

Making The Choice To Surrender

As a recovering control freak, I can tell you that the best thing I ever did was....... let go! I held on to the reigns of control like a rider in the Kentucky Derby feeling like if I released it would all come crashing around me. I couldn't see that I was pulling everything down around me as I was holding on with white knuckles. Swinging back and forth on a hopeless self braided rope of fear and insecurity that dangled in dead air with no ledge to land on. Finally, I looked past myself to see the Father waiting for me to give Him the ropes back. For me to realize that He could do a much better job with everything than I could. My release was the key to my receiving of freedom and of the joy that followed trust in the Father.

Today's challenge, "Making the Choice to Surrender," could very well be the best choice we make through this entire journey to joy. Let's first take a look at what it means to surrender.

Surrender (English): to cease resistance to an enemy or opponent and submit to their authority; give up or hand over (a person, right, or possession), typically on compulsion or demand; abandon oneself entirely to (a powerful emotion or influence); give in to

Paradidomi (Greek for Surrender): to give into the hands (of another); to give over into (one's) power or use; to commit, to commend; to deliver verbally; to permit allow

When we surrender, we place what we have into the hands of a most qualified authority. We commit those things to the Father in submission and abandon ourselves for the sake of the bigger picture. It takes trust. It takes courage. It takes action. This is where we stand. At the jumping point of action. I am calling all of us to take a deep breath, consider the Savior who holds us and jump into surrender with our arms in the air.

"Cast your burden on the Lord, and He will sustain you; He will never permit the righteous to be moved." Psalm 55:22 ESV

Find a quiet moment and honestly evaluate the things that have sat on your shoulders and need to be surrendered to the Lord. We aren't built to carry it all, and we don't have to. Choose to surrender it all today.

Prayer:

Lord, I give You all the praise for who You are. Thank You, God, for Your patience with me. I choose today to surrender all my burdens, desires, plans, and concerns to You. Help me to let go and trust Your plans. Increase my faith as I release control and trust You to do what's best for me. In Jesus Name AMEN!!!

My Journey

What area in my life have I held back from God?

What areas of my life have I allowed fear to creep in?

What, if anything, has made it hard for me to release fear?

What "junk" have I allowed to take up space in my life where God could bless?

What burdens do I need to transfer ownership of?

Discussion Questions

What did I learn about myself in this section?

What Scriptures stood out to me in this section?

What life application do I intend to implement with the discoveries that I have made?

Journaling Page

_____

_____

_____

_____

_____

_____

_____

_____

_____

_____

_____

_____

_____

_____

_____

_____

_____

_____

_____

_____

_____

_____

Part 4

Adjust Your Lens

One of the most irritating things in the world is having an eyelash in your eye and not being able to see it. You lift your eyelid, you have someone blow in it, you put water in it, and then miraculously it's no longer an issue. You're so relieved that you don't even care why it's better. You're just happy to see again.

We are blinded constantly by things that we don't even know are there let alone how they got there. We walk around with these proverbial eyelashes in our eyes, seemingly unbothered. The effects of the lack of sight are very evident. Lies, emotions, sin, confusion, pride, all these things cause us to be spiritually visually impaired.

The "D" Word

Some of us have been drowning in it for years and don't even know it is there (and no the "D" word is not drowning). This word has kept so many of us from achieving goals, growing spiritually, or even being able to experience life in its fullness. Oh, that wretched "D" word, **DENIAL!**

Denial: **1.** A refusal to comply with or satisfy a request. **2. a.** A refusal to grant the truth of a statement or allegation; a contradiction. **b.** *Law* The formal challenge by a defendant of the truth of an allegation made by the plaintiff. **3. a.** A refusal to accept or believe something, such as a doctrine or belief. **b.** *Psychology* An unconscious defense mechanism characterized by refusal to acknowledge painful realities, thoughts, or feelings.

We will take a closer look at the second part of that definition, to uncover the lies and detriment attached to this word. This word, unfortunately, has a sort of a twisted relevance for some of us. The problem with denial is that we generally don't know we are in denial because we are too busy denying.

Denial is a lie. A lie that you tell yourself so that you can either continue to live your life without guilt or continue to live life in a false reality. But guess what? This lie is what will keep you unhappy, unhealed, unsettled, and unsatisfied. Not facing the fact that we are responsible for some happenings in our life or refusing to see the truth around us will keep us bound and tied to where we are. True happiness can only come when we are willing to face the truth about the circumstances in our life, past and present. Living in denial is very dangerous to our future and present wellbeing. It keeps us in a holding place. It creates a kind of boiling pot of built up emotion and mental anguish and, when denial runs out and we have to face the somber music, we are usually not prepared. Shortly after, we are looking in to the face of depression, anger and an array of emotional damage. Facing our personal issues head on and being honest with ourselves eradicates the lie and keeps us from carrying unnecessary baggage.

We are responsible for our own contributions to every situation we are put against.

Lying to ourselves only makes recovery longer and tougher. We must face the hard truth that, yes, we are the reason for the choices we make, and yes, the situation is what we hoped it wouldn't be. But that's okay! Because once we have taken off the rose colored glasses, we can see the path to change and freedom. Opening up to the possibility of true unbridled honest self-examination can expose the hidden source that spawned the lies associated with denial. Taking a step back to look at the naked truth can help us release and move forward. We must pray for grace to deal with our issues honestly and realistically. It doesn't happen overnight but today's a great day to start the journey.

Study Verse- John 8:32 NIV

"Then you will know the truth, and the truth will set you free."

Where Is Your Focus?

Once my feet hit the ground in the morning, they are in a full-on 6-hour sprint to complete an extended list of things to do. There's chores, school, sewing, not to mention the 5 small off spring that reside in our home. All of which are in need of one thing or another for pretty much the entirety of the day. For some odd reason, we have to actually feed and attend to the children we have. They don't just come satisfied. How inconvenient, right? But seriously, why do they all have a need at the same exact time? It's like they go away and plot and then attack all at once. Help me Lord!

Needless to say, it can be pretty difficult to hone in and focus on what God has in front of me with so much going on. It's so easy to get distracted by our "oh so important" daily lives. We are pulled in so many directions and our focus gets cloudy at times. Well, today is going to be the first day of the rest of our lives. Today we are going to prioritize. We are going to wipe the plate clean and start putting the most important pieces on the plate first, the vegetables. By vegetables, I mean whatever is most healthy for us to consume spiritually, our consumption of Christ in our daily walk. Above all else our attention should first be pointed up. Our heavenly Father should be our focus all the time and in all things. When we take our eyes off of Him, is when things start to go all willy-nilly. Don't you remember Peter? He walked on water, but as soon as he took his eyes off Jesus, down he went (Matthew 14:27-31). If we take our eyes off of Him, our plans don't succeed. As soon as we think we need to change focus to what we want to be successful in, we actually lose out.

So what is it that steals our eyes? What continues to take the #1 spot so much so that we have a hard time trying to look up? In Peter's case, I would imagine that it was **fear** that stole his attention. This is also the case for some of us. In other instances it may be ambition, control, idolization, monetary gain, social status, and a plethora of other shiny things that have fought to stay in front. Unveiling the space holder of your main focus can be eye opening and sometimes painful. However, it's necessary for us to open that can of worms in order to really make that space available to Christ for His Lordship.

Similar to uncovering denial, getting to the truth about your spiritual and mental focus means that we have to be unrelenting with honesty in our self-evaluations. It may actually work best to get out a piece of paper and write out your thoughts during this process. Seeing myself on paper has always helped me to process the newly discovered information about myself. Think carefully about the things that you look to achieve during the course of the day. Look a little closer at each item and think about why you do these things and what is driving you to do the things that you have listed. Think also about where you see God in each of these activities and whether or not you have given Him space to be the Lord of each area. I would say that this exercise is crucial during our journey to the complete joy that Christ has for us. Where Christ is Lord, His joy is also present.

Our misdirected focuses rob us of the freedom God offers us in a life totally surrendered to Christ. Understanding what those focus stealers are, will allow us to stop them from stealing eye contact before we are lost.

Our number one focus should be pulled from the new life that we have been given. Having a God-focus in all aspects of our lives, whether that be in serving our children and raising them in the fear of the Lord, in the way we treat our employees or in the way we honor our spouse. *"Look to the Lord and His strength; seek His face always"* 1 Chronicles 16:11. When we choose to put our energy into the active pursuit of Christ, He takes over the areas that need attention. The word addresses this very clearly. *"The man who loves his life will lose it, while the man who hates his life in this world will keep it for eternal life. Whoever serves me must follow me; and where I am, my servant also will be. My Father will honor the one who serves me."* John 12:25-26 NIV. He has left many examples for us in the Bible.

We already have the instructions to this life. All we have to do is read them and put them to use. Don't get so lost in your own heart's desire that you forget about your Fathers heart. He knows our hearts desires and He is very generous.

Study Verse - Hebrews 12:1-2 NLT

"Therefore, since we are surrounded by such a huge crowd of witnesses to the life of faith, let us strip off every weight that slows us down, especially the sin that so easily trips us up. And let us run with endurance the race God has set before us. We do this by keeping our eyes on Jesus, the champion who initiates and perfects our faith. Because of the joy awaiting him, he endured the cross, disregarding its shame. Now he is seated in the place of honor beside God's throne."

Shifting Priorities ....

For the average adult, life is busy with many different focuses and directional pulls. We prioritize our lives and get them situated on our calendars and agendas, hoping that we can accomplish our goals in the least stressful fashion. But let's stop for a second and think about where God fits into those priorities. Does He get a space on the calendar? Is He even one of your priorities? Or has He been getting the leftovers?

How confused we have become in our culture when it comes to what's important in life. We have replaced God's #1 spot with work, exercise, kids, hobbies, even our social lives. These things that have never died for us, given us breath or provided life for us in any way. So why is it so easy for us to allow everything to take God's place in our lives? The Bible tells us that if we just look to the Lord, everything else will be fine. *"But seek first his kingdom and his righteousness, and all these things will be given to you as well."* Matthew 6:33 NIV. However somewhere in our flesh we just can't catch on to that at times. Not realizing that we sabotage ourselves by choosing agenda over the Lord and His presence.

Do you notice that most people, who are really successful in their career, usually are not successful all across the board? In most circumstances they are not successful in relationships, with money management or some other area in their life. Maybe this is a real issue for you. It could be that you are so focused on a problem in your life that consumes you. It's the same concept as with Peter. He was walking on water successfully when he had his eyes fixed on Jesus but as soon as he started to focus on the water and the storm around him, he began to sink. *"Let us fix our eyes on Jesus, the author and perfecter of our faith..."* Hebrews 12:2 NIVUK. When we keep our eyes on the Lord, He keeps His eyes on us (Luke 16:13). And with that He keeps His eyes on what we want/need and ensures that we are prosperous in all we do. *"The Lord will fight for you; you need only to be still."* Exodus 14:14 NIV.

The success of each day generally depends on how we prioritize and manage our time. If we can shift our focus toward heaven, making God the first priority on the schedule, we can have greater success with our other priorities. *"Set your minds on things above, not on earthly things"* Colossians 3:2 NIV. The things that seem so important in our daily lives here on earth have no value unless they bring glory and honor to our Lord and Savior. Putting God first in everything reaps benefits that transcends into our eternal life. But leaving Him out makes everything like dust.

I challenge all of us to be grateful and remember who gave us a life to prioritize in the first place. Let's remember Him in everything and make our best effort to make our God the #1 priority, all the time. Watch how the Lord will bless you.

Study Verse- Psalm 119:2 NIV

"Blessed are those who keep his statutes and seek him with all their heart"

Don't Follow Your Heart Just Yet

In our world, we have a "follow your heart" mentality that gives us the misled belief that we are supposed to do whatever feels good to us. Though this sounds like the correct way of thinking and it sounds like it's not harmful, that is far from the truth. Our hearts can easily be deceived by our fleshly nature. Which means that our hearts can easily have sinful desires that are harmful to us. If we do not make a conscience effort to let our hearts be controlled by the Holy Spirit, we will constantly be redirected to our sinful nature. We cannot be of the world and of the Spirit. The two cannot co-exist within us. One or the other will have an upper hand in your life.

"For the flesh desires what is contrary to the Spirit, and the Spirit what is contrary to the flesh. They are in conflict with each other, so that you are not to do whatever you want." Galatians 5:17 NIV.

Our natural instinct is to go against the will of God. Therefore we are left to choose to direct our will in the right direction. It is a choice to give control of our lives to the Lord in order to become righteous and holy. It is impossible to lead a complete God-centered life by our own hands. We know not what we truly need or what the Lord truly wants for us. The only way to live a complete life is through surrendered control. Surrendering your will to the Holy Spirit will align you with God's will, freeing you up to receive the rewards of the righteous and the fruit of the Spirit.

Study Verse- Romans 8:8 NIV

"Those who are in the realm of the flesh cannot please God."

Not My Thoughts

Our dreams can be larger than life. We often find that one thing we consider to be exactly what we want out of life and hang onto it and hardly waver from the original thought of that dream. Sometimes we even obsess over these dreams and dedicate our lives to them, giving us a sort of tunnel vision and often also creating stress and anxiety. So, when things don't go according to the map that we have laid out in our heads, we get flustered and can't seem to grasp why our dream is not what we thought it would be or why it hasn't arrived when we thought it should.

Well, I have some dreams of my own that I had been thinking over and realized that I was just wasting time worrying about them. God knows all of my dreams, and all of my desires, so why would I spend any amount of time being consumed by them. If I can have faith for the small stuff, even some big stuff that I don't feel any need to control, why can't I have the same faith about my dreams that I "think" I have control over. Not just mediocre, "I know He is going to take care of it" faith, but "He's thought about it already, so why should I worry" type faith.

This contemplating session led me to Isaiah 55:8 *"My thoughts are nothing like your thoughts," says the Lord. "and my ways are far beyond anything you could imagine."* After reading this Scripture, I thought about the things that God has done: created the earth, man from dust, and so on. The word "imagine" really made me think about the comparison between our human imagination and God's almighty imagination.

The seemingly glorious dreams, though in comparison lackluster, that we seam together could be so much more. If God's mind could think up all that it has, imagine what He could do for our dreams and desires. If we would just give Him our dreams and say, "Father, let your will be done." We could never imagine the magnitude at which He could bring them to pass. Our father has our dreams tied into the plans He has for us, *"For I know the plans I have for you"* says the Lord. *,"They are plans of good and not disaster, to give you a future and a hope"* Jeremiah 29:11. If He can do it for Jeremiah, guess what, He can do it for us. Our Father has our best interest in mind and heart. He will not run out of goodness or good plans or wisdom or grace or power. His thinking is on a much bigger scale than ours and letting Him do the dreaming for us allows Him to make the outcome a whole lot better than our own planning could ever produce.

Release your big dreams. Hand them over to the Father and creator of dreams. Let Him worry about the details and timing and free yourself of the pressure of making your dreams come true on your own. It is done.

Study Verse- Proverbs 16:3
"Commit your actions to the Lord, and your plans will succeed."

Where are you looking for favor?

Measuring our happiness by worldly accomplishments and status is a common downfall today. Challenging ourselves to know more people, fit in with a select crowd or getting in good with the executives at the job so that we can feel good about ourselves. Once we get to that favored placed we wanted to be, we are still unfulfilled and hardly any happier than we were before. In some cases, you experience a lower level of joy and are less content or even depressed because of all the stress associated with trying to keep at the favored level. This completely blurs

112

the true meaning of happiness and success. Contradicting the biblical truths associated with actual joy and achievement.

In a world where getting approval and acceptance from your peers is almost encouraged, it can be hard to remember that we have no need for the approval of our fellow humans. We also have no need to search for favor with them beyond what the Lord has given. I know it can be hard to think that way when you are in a corporate setting and you may feel the need to be on every one's good side or feel like you need to adjust yourself to receive favor from the people around you, often forgetting your salvation. But looking to the one who gives favor from on high will always keep you in good favor. *"For those who find me find life and receive favor from the Lord."* Proverbs 8:35 NIV.

Favor from people is very conditional. You have to work hard enough or dress nice enough or act proper enough. All that and you will still have no true reward at the end of it all. Just meaningless clout. Favor from our Father in heaven is a long lasting reward that can reach every area of our lives. *"For his anger lasts only a moment, but his favor lasts a lifetime; weeping may stay for the night, but rejoicing comes in the morning."* Psalm 30:5 NIV. When God pours out His favor on us, it reaches our home life, ministry life, and work life, and it all comes from one source.

Shifting our eyes to the true giver of favor reaps all the desired benefits of mistakenly seeking favor in a peer and more. Narrow your thoughts toward leading a righteous life and favor will come as a byproduct.

Study Verse- Psalm 5:12 NIV

"Surely, Lord, you bless the righteous; you surround them with your favor as with a shield."

Seeing the Light…..

There are times when we come to what seems like a corner in life. We feel like we have been obedient and we have done things right but it seems like your just stuck. You know like one of those wind-up toys that has made it's way to the corner of a room, and the legs are just walking nowhere. Stuck emotionally, spiritually and sometimes even physically. These stages of life can make us feel many of different ways about where we are and who we are. Feelings of inadequacy or uncertainty can begin to surface when we are facing the corner. These are the moments that test our spiritual maturity. This is also when the enemy tries his best tactics on us. However, trusting the Father when nothing seems right is the ultimate testimony and strengthening exercise for our faith. *"O LORD of Heaven's Armies, what joy for those who trust in you"* Psalm 84:12 NLT.

I know, seeing the light at the end of the tunnel when you feel like you're looking at a dark corner can be very difficult. Especially because facing that dark corner is very discouraging and can sometimes feel hopeless. Trying to remember a cliché quote about seeing the light is generally not the first thing that comes to mind when we are battling to get out of where we are. One thing we can remember is Who our light is and put our hope in Him. *"We put our hope in the LORD. He is our help and our shield. "* Psalm 33:20 NLT. Our hope in Him is our floaty when we feel like we are drowning. It's the light that we follow out of the tunnel. While we wait on the Lord, His word will sustain us.

Knowing that His truth never fails is the key to keeping your joy and sanity when life looks bleak. We have to hold on to God's promises while trusting that He knows what He's doing.

Study Verse- Psalm 12:6 NLT

"The LORD's promises are pure, like silver refined in a furnace, purified seven times over.

CHOICE CHALLENGE #4 :

Making the Choice to LOOK

I'm sure you've heard the term, "Looking through rose-colored glasses". If you haven't, let me take a few moments to explain. This saying simply means that a person can only see the good they want to see and not what's really happening right before their eyes. For example, a parent of a teenager could choose to believe that her child is just experiencing a small stint of hyperactiveness, rather than see the truth that their son is actually using speed on a regular basis. For the sake of this challenge we'll call it the "Rose Glasses Syndrome". It is also known as denial in most parts of the world. This issue can keep us in a numb state of mind for an extended period of time creating a false reality.

For this reason, we are "Making the Choice to LOOK" today. And, I mean really, LOOK and see what's happening in and around us. This challenge is probably going to take you to places in your mind that you thought you didn't have and may lead you to eliminate things that you thought weren't harmful. For this challenge, you are going to need paper, lots of prayer and probably a tissue or two depending on how deep you get.

Our main focus for today's exercise is to look at our lives with an honest eye. We are going to think about our motives, our intentions and the things that we involve ourselves in day-to-day. *"Because of the privilege and authority God had given me, I give each of you this warning. Don't think you are better than you really are. Be honest in your evaluation of yourselves, measuring yourselves by the faith God has given us."* Romans 12:3 NLT. This Scripture is crystal clear. No mystical talk here. Paul is keeping it straight forward as he writes these instructions to the Christians of Rome. Before this he is giving other Christian life instructions, such as, *"Being a living and holy sacrifice"* and *"Don't copy the behavior and customs of this world"* (Romans 12:1-2 NLT).

As we take an honest LOOK at ourselves today, we are going to write down and pray about the parts we haven't seen clearly. The parts that don't look very much like the other instructions Paul has written throughout Romans 12. Be encouraged throughout this process, my friends, because the grace and mercy of God is still fresh and available to cover and redeem those places that we have only experienced with the "Rose Glass Syndrome". As we take the glasses off to look closely and honestly, allow Christ to make the necessary adjustments for healing and cleansing. Claim David's song as your own today, *"Create in me a clean heart, O God. Renew a loyal spirit in me."* Psalm 51:10 NLT.

"Instead, let the Spirit renew your thoughts and attitudes." Ephesians 4:23 NLT.

"and to be renewed in the spirit of your minds," Ephesians 4:23 ESV

Prayer:

Lord Jesus, I praise You for having thoughts different than my own. Help me to see clearly so that I can focus on Your will for me. Give me the wisdom I need to make good choices that reflect Your heart. Create in me a clean and righteous spirit that glorifies You. Thank You, Father. In Jesus name, Amen!

My Journey

What areas in my life has denial kept me from growing?

What things have I allowed to steal my focus?

What areas in my life do I struggle to see the light?

Discussion Questions

What did I learn about myself in this section?

What Scriptures stood out to me in this section?

What life application do I intend to implement with the discoveries that I have made?

Journaling Page

Part 5

Apples and Onions......I mean, Oranges

This stop in our journey is one that I believe to be another critical stop on our way to living in Christ's lasting joy. Knowing the differences between the apples and the oranges (sometimes onions). Brace yourself.

Decisions, Decisions…..

Remember that saying, "What Would Jesus Do?" It was like a phrase epidemic in the 90's. It was everywhere and on everything. It was a little corny, but I love it because this is exactly what we should think when we are making decisions in our daily walk. Even though most times that question is more like "What

Should I Do?" In our everyday life we face many different choices to make. From what we want to eat for breakfast to where we want to sit on the subway. Beyond those trivial choices we make daily, we face moral choices like whether we should be honest or tell a lie when we are in a challenging situation. The choices we make create a certain path for us. We can choose to go down the path of self-loathing and pity or we can choose to go down the road of Christ's peace and comfort. We can chose to walk down the narrow road of Godliness or go down the wide path of sinfulness. Then, there are the less obvious decisions to be made, like the decision to share the gospel with a friend or not. For most Christians, the road can often have a few detours and forks. So let's examine why we make the choices we make.

For most of us, the things that we've experienced have in some way shaped our opinions and moral judgment. For me, in my early adulthood, many of my decisions we based on the lives that surrounded me. Sometimes even though we know that something we are doing goes completely against the word of God, we can justify why we have made a the choice to do it anyway. Unfortunately, the things that make us feel justified, will not excuse us from the consequences for making that bad choice. In some circumstances, we allow other people to choose for us or influence our choices. This is very risky because if we just go along with what someone else has chosen to do, we are still responsible for the choice. The Lord gave us the Holy Spirit to help us make the right choices not the people around us. Ignoring the wisdom and conviction of the Holy Spirit can lead to grave consequences and can even lessen your sensitivity to the whispers of Spirit.

We have to make a clear decision to live life as a conscience decider. Becoming a person of conscience living is quite simple. First we have to take responsibility for our own lives, our own relationship with Christ and the decisions we make. Then we must be honest with ourselves and honestly evaluate each situation so that we can make the best God honoring decision. Once we realize that we are the only ones accountable for the choices we make, true growth can happen and we can really head toward Christ's lasting joy. Everything we do should be lead by our Christ relationship, His Spirit and His word. So ask yourself, "What Would Jesus Do?"

Study Verse-1 Peter 2:21 NIV

"To this you were called, because Christ suffered for you, leaving you an example, that you should follow in his steps."

Mistakes vs. Choices

At random intervals of time I kind of give myself a spiritual self-examination. I sift through some of my deeds, my thoughts and my motives with a fine-toothed comb to see what areas I need to ask God to strengthen. I pay special attention to not forgetting to recognize the growth stunting thorns that I need to ask God to help me pull out. One time in particular led to me thinking about all the things I had done and I should not have done in life. I pondered all of the bad choices that I had made and mistakes I thought I had made. Then I started to think, "Were the mistakes I made really mistakes?" Could it be that I had just made a conscious decision to do what I knew was wrong? This plagued me quite a bit. I started to examine the words mistake, error and choose. Here's my discovery via the dictionary.

mis·take: **1.** An error or fault resulting from defective judgment, deficient knowledge, or carelessness. **2.** A misconception or misunderstanding.

error: **1.** An act, assertion, or belief that unintentionally deviates from what is correct, right, or true. **2.** The condition of having incorrect or false knowledge. **3.** The act or an instance of deviating from an accepted code of behavior. **4.** A mistake.

choose: **1.** To select from a number of possible alternatives; decide on and pick out: *Which book did you choose at the library?* **2. a.** To prefer above others: *chooses the supermarket over the neighborhood grocery store.* **b.** To determine or decide: *chose to fly rather than drive.*

In many of our minds the definition of mistake is similar to that of a bad choice. Though, generally, when we think of a mistake without it being attached to an actual circumstance, we think that people simply have done something that they didn't have intention to do. So, how is it that we come to the same conclusion when people make a bad choice in life? Even when they

124

clearly knew the consequences associated with that choice? Frequently we compassionately tell them it was just a mistake. We've all heard that excusing phrase, "We all make mistakes." But, what classifies as a mistake? Because in a lot of circumstances, it's not a mistake it's more like a bad choice. And, yes, we all make mistakes but, unfortunately, we all also make bad choices. Knowingly making the choice to sin is no mistake. It's just plain making the choice to sin.

Coming to a clarification of the differences between making mistakes and making choices can determine the outcome of our future circumstances. Recognizing when a mistake is really a bad choice, gives us the power to turn things around. It gives us a clear view of our playing field and takes out the fog of deception. It's helping us to take responsibility for our part, while keeping us accountable to our own behavior.

The Bible makes it clear that we can choose the right path. For example, in the following passages:

"Choose a good reputation over great riches; being held in high esteem is better than silver or gold." Proverbs 22:1 NLT

"Don't you realize that you become the slave of whatever you choose to obey? You can be a slave to sin, which leads to death, or you can choose to obey God, which leads to righteous living." Romans 6:16 NLT

"But those who choose their own ways— delighting in their detestable sins—will not have their offerings accepted..." Isaiah 66:3 NLT

Making conscious decisions will aid us in seeing the bigger picture instead of only the right now and not allowing the wrong influence to make a decision for us. Regardless of our stance in the truth about our decisions, we are held accountable to the so-called mistakes we make. Opening up to the possibility that our mistake was really a bad choice assists us in making a better choice the next time that circumstance arises. It will also bring us to a quicker repentance and rebound. Our true happiness depends solely on our choices. We have to choose Jesus, we have to choose to love one another, and we have to choose to make the God honoring choices. I challenge you to think a little harder before making your next "mistake". I know I will.

Study Verse - Proverbs 8:10 NLT

"Choose my instruction rather than silver, and knowledge rather than pure gold"

Birds of a Feather

While we are on the subject of choices, there's an area of our lives where our choice can linger into a life span, our choice of friends. Hanging out with good friends can be great for the spirit. Much of the time, it can be just what the doctor ordered; to clear our head and just let loose. I love a bang up girl's night like every other chick and I'm sure most men enjoy guy nights. Sharing open dialogue and swapping stories is always a pleasure in the hen house or man cave. However there is a sneaky enemy to the atmosphere of friendly banter because accompanying that pleasure can also be other things that are harmful. Like gossip, negativity, prideful attitudes, insecurities and selfish motives. We've all heard that lovely sentiment, "birds of a feather flock together." Growing up I would hear it from everyone in the generations before trying to warn us from getting too involved with the wrong crowd. Then, when I got older, I would catch myself saying it but I'm not sure I thought about what it really meant.

Taking a closer look at that quote, I decided to do a little research on poultry. I wanted to see what their behaviors were in order to understand the relevance of this famous quote for all of us. When geese migrate, they generally stick close together in a formation with other geese that are of the same species. You don't see geese migrating with swans. You also don't see an eagle hanging out in a nest with an owl. Why? Because they have different needs, purposes, appetites, and mating habits. So they really have no need to interact on a regular basis with each other even though they can still live in the same eco-system.

This funny but true bird quote can take shape in a variety of ways in our lives. Many of us may have never thought that our friends could be a contributing factor to our unhappiness/happiness. It's quite a hard pill to swallow when you realize that your friend of thirty years has been a roadblock on your journey to joy. Or maybe you have been someone else's stumbling block. The reality is that our friends have a bigger impact on our lives than we think. For instance, if you hang out with drug dealers, odds are that you are not a Bible sales-man unless you are making an active choice to minister to them. In most cases, your friends are a reflection of who you are, whether you know who you really are or not. As Christ's children we have a calling to be the example to the people around us, not the reflection of the people around us. The only one we should be reflecting and following is Christ.

The people we allow residence in our heart spaces, if not given boundaries, can make unhealthy deposits that we are not prepared to combat. It is so important to be careful whom we allow to make emotional deposits into us. It is critical to be very aware of the soul ties we make and set proper boundaries. Our minds have a tendency to weaken when we hold compassion or tender emotion for someone, which gives way for temptation to creep in and become sin.
This makes it imperative for us to stay alert.

An example of friendly influence is, if you have a friend who is always happy and positive, when you leave a shared time with that friend you feel good and positive. However, if you spend time with a friend who can only see the glass as half empty all the time, suddenly you will begin to feel unfulfilled and dissatisfied in your own life. You can be joyful one day and one conversation with the wrong person can put you on the fast track to "not so happy." With this type of friends, we have to limit interaction and try to let our positive over power the negative. Because if you are not quite sure where you stand, you can easily turn into that negative friend.

In some cases, you may have to do the hardest thing and allow the relationship cease. Though it can be extremely hard to let go of friends that you have had for years, and you may feel like you couldn't bear not to be in close relationship with them, that relationship could be blocking the joy that God is trying to give you. We have to draw a line in the sand and decide what we are willing to let cross the line. I am in no way saying that you have to lose all your old friends in order to live life. However, it may be time to take inventory of the influences you allow to mold you and where they come from. This may lead you to letting some people go or perhaps setting new boundaries. If you need to, just explain to them that you are moving in a positive direction for your life and you may have to pull back a little. A real friend will understand and probably hop on board to make an effort to improve their life. But if they are not supportive, just apologize and do your best to cordially move forward. Our relationship with Christ is more important than any other relationship and that relationship produces the lasting joy that we are in search of. Today I challenge you to examine your relationships and see where you need to "pull back". I encourage you to be honest with yourself and your friend(s).

Study Verse-Romans 8:6 NIV

"The mind governed by the flesh is death, but the mind governed by the Spirit is life and peace."

Housing a Criminal in Your Heart

Remember when we were kids and we would compare everything with each other? "I have bigger feet." "He has better toys." "They have more money." Blah blah blah blah. I remember when I was a kid, there was this one girl who seemed to always have bigger and better than just about everyone. I was so irritated every time she would bring out her new something or brag about something she had. For some reason it was like all the blessings that I had would just disappear when this chick would open her mouth. I hated feeling not good enough or like I didn't have enough to offer. Even though it was just pointless stuff, I still felt small in comparison.

COMPARISON......

It's the criminal we allow to set up tents in our hearts causing us to take shelter in discontentment. The enemy is a master illusionist. He blows all the great magicians out of the water. He's so talented at it that he doesn't really need to do much at all to deceive us and pull a whammy over on us. That doesn't stop the illusion from taking effect. One of his best card tricks is to show us what someone else has and what we don't. This trick is a not only deceiving but it's also quite consuming bringing about that ugly joy thief.

When we compare, we plant seeds of ungratefulness, greed, and envy where seeds of encouragement and contentment should be. We draw lines between us and people, between us and love, as well as between us and truth. *"Love is patient, love is kind. It does not envy, it does not boast, it is not proud." 1 Corinthians 13:4 NIV.* The result of all of this generally leads to sin. Ungratefulness grows the yeast of want and discontentment, making nothing good enough. Envy brings about malice, division, hatred, and vicious thoughts and actions. *"A heart at peace gives life to the body, but envy rots the bones." Proverbs 14:30 NIV*

What a shame! We allow comparison to steal not only our joy but also our view of God's truth about who we are. Comparison causes us to look around at what God has provided for others rather than what He has done for us. We willingly give comparison all the tools it needs to rob us of the joy that was meant for us. Our hearts become consumed with want and our minds become consumed with our lack rather than our position. We have got to stop the "Looky Looky" game. Besides, it isn't all that fun in the first place. It's like self-torture.

Instead of thinking, "look what they have," we must try "look what I have," "look whose I am," "look where I've come from."

Identifying and carrying the truth of our position in Christ allows us to house welcomed guests in our hearts. What the Holy Spirit produces in us is, joy, love, peace, and hope. From a heart guided by the Spirit, we can sewn the seeds of the Spirit.

Study Verse- Galatians 6:4-8 ESV

"But let each one test his own work, and then his reason to boast will be in himself alone and not in his neighbor. For each will have to bear his own load. Let the one who is taught the word share all good things with the one who teaches. Do not be deceived: God is not mocked, for whatever one sows, that will he also reap. For the one who sows to his own flesh will from the flesh reap corruption, but the one who sows to the Spirit will from the Spirit reap eternal life."

He Loves Us Too Much To Leave Us…..

Warning: Difficult topic coming up!

Now that we have grit our teeth through the last couple sections, I figured you are probably prepped good for what we're going to tackle next. You may want to grab a glass of water and take a few deep cleansing breaths before you read on.

Let's do it together…..

Breathe in….. 1-2-3-4

Breathe out…..1-2-3-4

Ok…….Let's do this!

What's one of the most frightening words in the English language?

CHANGE!!!

People hear that word and immediately go into sheer panic at the thought of being shifted from their comfort zone a little. For what reason? I'm not sure because most of our comfort zones are pretty pathetic, although comfy as they may be.

Change: 1. a. To cause to be different: *change the spelling of a word.* **b.** To give a completely different form or appearance to; transform: *changed the yard into a garden.* **2.** To give and receive reciprocally; interchange: *change places.* **3.** To exchange for or replace with another, usually of the same kind or category: *change one's name; a light that changes colors.* **4. a.** To lay aside, abandon, or leave for another; switch: *change methods; change sides.* **b.** To transfer from (one conveyance) to another: *change planes*

None of those definitions sound scary, but that doesn't keep people from being so afraid of change that it cripples their progress in life. The thing people fail to realize, or refuse to face, is that life can't get better without change. We try to keep living our same sad lives and thinking it will just get better somehow. This makes no sense! Albert Einstein said it best with his definition of insanity: "Insanity: Doing the same thing over and over again expecting different results". There is no way that life will just get better without an active attempt to do better on our part.

There are lots of great things that can happen with change. Especially when we are changing in obedience to Gods Word. The Father delights in us and wants to see us do well in life and delight in Him. But also, just like every great father, He must correct us and show us the right way to go. *"I correct and discipline everyone I love. So be diligent and turn from your indifference"* Revelation 3:19 NLT.

At times, some of us feel like following God's instruction takes away what we want. This is only a one-sided, disillusioned view. True, you may need to let go of some of your sinful habits that you think mean the world. But look at it this way, would you rather have that little bit of pleasure (that brings death and condemnation in the long run) for that moment or have true joy that will last for a lifetime and a guilt free conscience. The guilt of living a life covered in the filth that should have been washed off in salvation, especially when you are aware of your sinful indulgences, is such a pointless, heavy burden. Doing the death dance with sin has never created an atmosphere of peace where joy runs free. This is why we are commanded to repent and go in the opposite direction. *"Now repent of your sins and turn to God, so that your sins may be wiped away."* Acts 3:19 NLT.

Repent: **1.** To feel remorse, contrition, or self-reproach for what one has done or failed to do; be contrite:

Our testimony shines best when we submit to a radical change through Christ. Once we have repented and made Christ the Lord of our lives, the next steps are releasing our old lives (as we bury it in the water of baptism), picking up the new life and turning to go forward in the direction of Christ. Take a look at the first disciples, Simon (also called Peter) and Andrew, they dropped everything to follow Jesus. *"Now as Jesus was walking by the Sea of Galilee, He saw two brothers, Simon who was called Peter, and Andrew his brother, casting a net into the sea; for they were fishermen. And He said to them, "Follow Me, and I will make you fishers of men." Immediately they left their nets and followed Him."* Matthew 4:18-20. This story is a clear picture of what it should look like once we enter into relationship with Jesus. Total abandon and obedience.

135

They abandoned what they had known to follow after what they had yet to know. This life on earth will be gone in the blink of an eye but our eternal life (which we receive at salvation) is exactly that, ETERNAL! So wouldn't you think that it makes more since to be more concerned about that life, which can either be spent where there are streets of gold or where there is eternal burning with no water and gnashing of teeth?

We can't get caught up in the lies that the world has to offer, telling us that we should do whatever feels good to us. Ultimately, what feels good to you now may not feel so good later. *"My child, if sinners entice you, turn your back on them!"* Proverbs 1:10 NLT. Nothing we do is not known to God and He is watching our world crumble at the hands of sin and very sad I'm sure. Just imagine watching your kids walking off cliff after cliff when you have already warned them about it. You would still try to stop them, as you sobbed and watch in horror as they fell. I'd imagine our heavenly Father experiencing this everyday? I urge you to rethink the direction in which your life is going. We cannot have a blessed life if we are willingly diving into sin. Nothing will ever seem to be going right if we know better and still chose our own way. Life on earth is just too short to settle for an un-blessed, guilt ridden, unhappy life. We were made to be so much more. Please pray on this subject and allow the Spirit of God to revamp your life so that you can experience His security and blessing where ever you go. Let's make the **CHANGE**!

Study Verse- Matthew 3:8 NLT (also read verses 9-11)

"Prove by the way you live that you have repented of your sins and turned to God."

Putting Your Best Linemen On The Field

"A prudent person foresees danger and takes precautions. The simpleton goes blindly on and suffers the consequences." Proverbs 27:12 NLT

In football, most great teams have incredible defensive linemen. Like running brick walls, they are on the move to stop anything, a man, a ball, or a squirrel, from getting past them. Why? They know that if they can stop the other team from scoring, they won't have to worry about losing. They know that the less points the other team scores, the more likely they are to win. The opposing team, on the other hand is usually trying to figure out the best way to get around the star defensive linemen, looking for holes in the wall they can get through in order to get the score. This is what the enemy does with us. He is constantly on the look out for holes in our defensive wall to get the score. And, if we aren't using our best linemen, we can loose the game.

When we forget that the "best defense is a good offense", we leave the playing field up to chance instead of giving ourselves the better odds. Our defense strategy against the enemy cannot be left up to chance or hopefulness. We must ready ourselves to stand against the schemes and devices of the enemy by putting our best defense up. Setting boundaries makes it easier to walk out a life of faith. When we make efforts to protect ourselves from the enemy, by blocking the holes he comes through, we set ourselves up to win.

A person who deals with a pornography issue should probably not have much access to the Internet or cable TV. A person who has an addiction problem should likely not spend much time where those habits are fed. When we foresee the sin, we are obligated to head it off with all we have. *"The simple believes everything, but the prudent gives thought to his steps. One who is wise is cautious and turns away from evil, but a fool is reckless and careless."* Proverbs 14:15-16 ESV. Creating new patterns, finding accountability in a friend, surrounding yourself with people of faith, cutting off the funnel where sin drips in, and changing perspective, are all actions that create boundaries to set us up for the win. Looking at our life and asking, "If I keep living how I'm living now, where will I be?" may be a little scary for some of us but it may be the question we need to ask in order to see the reality of our circumstance. Then we can make a sufficient strategy and game plan that will block the enemy from making the score and bust our chances for the WIN.

If we ask ourselves that question and be truly honest with the answer, we could possibly make radically effective adjustments that could change the direction of our lives. What are you doing with your life right now?

What boundaries have you set to protect your faith? Do you see yourself being where you believe the will of God would have you in 5 years or so doing life how you are doing it right now? If you have no answer to these questions, it's possible that you may need to make some changes in your current lifestyle patterns and the boundaries (or lack thereof) you have set. Our faith is precious, our salvation is precious, and the life we have been gifted is precious and we must guard these gifts from the Father. He has already laid out the path and is directing us, however, we have to use the wisdom and faith He has given us to follow His will. He has already made a way for us to prosper and have joy. We just have to tell the devil to take his hands off of what's yours, rebuke his curse from that which is yours, and trust God.

The Lord never intended for us to be broken, depressed, lost, and confused. He also never intended for us to waste our money, follow the ways of the world, blaspheme His name or walk away from Him. A life lived laid bare to the world is a life not protected. A life lived covered by the Father is a life that flourishes. His Word and His Spirit teach us how to take precautions that will protect us.

The Father wants us to be winners in this life, from an eternal perspective. Winning is not how much accolades you can collect here on earth. Winning is living a life in Christ, through Christ, for Christ. He created us to walk out life according to the will that He intended for us as He joins with us on the same accord.

If how we live is outside of the Lord's intended will, we cannot expect Him to bless the life that we have created without Him.

In order for the Holy Spirit to achieve all that He wants to within us, we must resolve to make choices that do not grieve Him (Ephesians 4:30-31; 1Thessalonians 5:19-22). Our lives are best lived when we use them as a worship offering to the Father. When we set ourselves up to hear from Him, our spirit aligns with His and we gain right perspectives. Pray and ask God to show you His best defensive strategy for your life. Watch how He grows your faith through your pursuit of holiness. The Lord wants to operate through us but we must be willing. He is gentle and will not force us into submission but waits patiently with arms full of grace to wrap us in. We must walk toward those arms. Get to a quiet place and listen to the Father. That one act can set the course for an entire adventure.

Living a life driven by the Holy Spirit is the greatest precaution you can take. Letting your life be led by the Word is our best defense against the enemy.

I challenge you to be honest with yourself. Are you taking the necessary precautions to have a healthy faith based life covered by Christ? If not, write down things that you may need to get rid of in your life that are counter-productive to having a life that honors God. Pray about those areas. Next, write the necessary steps you need to take to place proper boundaries and start in the right direction. Pray for strength and focus.

Track your changes and positive effects from taking spiritual precaution.

CHOICE CHALLENGE #5:

Making the Choice to Choose

I know that this has been a tough section to swallow, the thought of a challenge right now may be a little daunting but His grace is sufficient to carry us forward. Take some time to reflect on what we have covered in this last section, and then take a deep breath and jump right back into this choice challenge.

Our challenge: "Making the Choice to Choose". The choice to CHOOSE Jesus in every circumstance. By "choosing Jesus" I mean, intentionally choosing His ways in all we do.

We can easily select small areas that we struggle with in our personal lives and be determined to make a change to go in a different direction in that area. Our scope of things can get narrow and we can simply forget the reason we do things in the first place. Sure, it's great for us to make small changes. That's how the big changes usually come to pass. But I'm thinking a little deeper than that. If all of our choices stemmed from one major choice, choosing Jesus, making the small choices that collectively make the big change would be easier.

Remember that 90's saying we talked about, "What Would Jesus Do"? So corny right? Yet so valuable! If we would just sit on that thought before acting and reacting, we would probably have a lot more peace and a lot less mistakes. As Christians we bare His name and are by definition called to be "Christ like". So what does that look like? Does that mean that we are only called to be Christ like on Sundays when people are watching and expect us to be holy? I think not. That's like only being an American on the 4th of July. Not really an option. We carry the name of Christ and are therefore charged with the responsibility of walking like citizens of heaven under the authority of Christ *("But there is one thing I want you to know; The head of every man is Christ, the head of woman is man and the head of Christ is God."* 1Corinthians 11:3 NLT).

Today we are going to look Jesus directly in the face and choose His ways above our own. His will above our want. His flawless righteousness over our fleshly regard. Let's choose His attitude, His patience, His humility, His heart and His grace. *"You must have the same attitude that Christ had. Though He was equal to God, He did not think of equality with God as something to cling to. Instead, He gave up His divine privileges He took the humble position of a slave and was born as a human being. When He appeared in human form, He humbled himself in obedience to God and died a criminals death on a cross."* Philippians 2:5-8NLT. This is the picture of what it means to follow Christ. Yes, we are royalty of heaven and heir with Christ Jesus, but we are also called to FOLLOW Christ Jesus in His humility and service unto the world.

"For God called you to do good, even if it means suffering, just as Christ suffered for you. He is your example, and you must follow in His steps." 1 Peter 2:21NLT.

Be encouraged that He is not asking you to do it alone. Choosing Him also means that you have Him to walk with on the journey. So we are going to make it real simple today. CHOOSE Jesus! No matter what CHOOSE JESUS!

Prayer:

Lord Jesus, thank You for Your flawless example. I give You all the glory for the steps You have taken before me. Lord, clear our vision so that I can look You in the face without obstruction. Show me Your ways O Lord that I would walk in the steps that You have set before me. Today I surrender my flesh to You, Jesus. I surrender personal gain and selfish motivation to You. We surrender the right to be right. I surrender my thoughts and language to You, Jesus. And I take on Your light burden. God, I thank You for the freedom that comes in choosing You in all I do. In Jesus Name Amen!!!

My Journey

What bad choices have I made that I mask as mistakes?

What relationships have I allowed to make unhealthy deposits?

Are there things in my life that I have not repented for that are taking up space and possibly taking root? (Please take the time to repent so that you can be free from that burden.)

Where have I allowed pride to stunt my growth in Christ?

Discussion Questions

What did I learn about myself in this section?

What Scriptures stood out to me in this section?

What life application do I intend to implement with the discoveries that I have made?

Journaling Page

Part 6

Camping in the Winter

Suffering in Season

Suffering has as many faces as people in the world. Everyone experiences tribulation of some kind during their life here on earth. Some sufferings are obvious, some secret, some self-imposed, some people imposed, some temporary, some permanent and the list goes on. Our world is drowning in sorrow and suffering on a daily basis. We all have our fair share of tribulation to juggle along with the rest of life.

"If I can just make it to bed" was the thought that would swirl around in my head throughout the day as I was trying to calm myself down. My heart racing and my body temperature fluctuating like I was in prime menopause mode or something. Fighting back tears as I stood at the counter slathering peanut butter on my third PB&J suppressing every urge to throw it clear across the room. I wanted to scream, cry, hide, and run out of my own skin all at the same time just to escape the feeling I was having. I couldn't breathe and I felt like I was losing my mind with no way to express it. Anxiety. I was caught completely off guard. How could this be my reality? "I can handle anything," I thought. I had no idea what to do, so I hid it. No one knew that I was suffering silently with terrifying feelings of being completely out of control. Every episode a nightmare.

My experience with anxiety, though an on and off ordeal throughout life, still has its assigned seasons. Like most seasons of suffering, it seems to last forever until it's over. For some of us, suffering could look like sickness, grief, living in fear, anxiety, depression, hardship and so many other circumstances that bring us to a place of darkness. These chunks of life are breath taking in a not so great way and can leave us desperate and grasping at anything that looks like relief even if it's really just taking us deeper into the abyss that we are in. Suffering can bring us to places we never thought we would go. It can take us to places that prompt us to question God and ourselves and everyone around us. When we walk into a patch of suffering we are immediately thrown off balance. Confusion strikes and we have a million questions Why. Our psyche automatically tries to make sense of it all using our puny human logic, making us even more confused. We become irrational, vulnerable, and disheveled. Most importantly, we become moldable.

Although moldable is great, when we're in the trenches it's not exactly the first thing on our mind. Now, I think it's safe to say that on a more than a regular basis, I am a pretty positive lady. However, in several spans of seasonal transition, I've been evaluating my reaction to situations in particular seasons of my life. Although overall I am enjoying the life I have been given, I find that I have taken opportunities to complain about the "unpleasants" during my personal seasons of suffering and allowed myself to take refuge in the emotions (a totally inadequate place of refuge) that came with those different seasons of life. I felt entitled to the choices I was making out of emotions and pride, as if I had the right to be upset/irritated and to let it be known to God and others.

My complaints and fits of rage did nothing to add any amount of delight to my circumstances in the least. If anything, they just seemed to put a bitter taste on my pallet, causing ungratefulness, confusion, weariness, and discontent to settle in. While I thought that I was justified in my righteous anger and complaints, I was actually planting seeds of resentment and bitterness that could have taken deep root.

Making my emotions and self-righteousness my refuge was a huge mistake. Emotions are shifty at best and self-righteousness is a joke because our "self" has no righteousness at all.

Yes, I know it's perfectly human to feel the sting of suffering, take a few complaining jabs at life, and maybe make a few disgruntle inquiries to the Father. We are so blessed that God is patient with us as we unleash the floodgates of disgust and anger. He can totally handle our worst and waits for us with compassion as we make our way through confusion, fear, and trust issues. I also know that the Word of God calls us to do the opposite and rejoice in those times. *"And not only this, but we also exult in our tribulations, knowing that tribulation brings about perseverance; and perseverance, proven character; and proven character, hope; and hope does not disappoint, because the love of God has been poured out within our hearts through the Holy Spirit who was given to us." Romans 5:3-5 NASB.* We don't have to look at it in a negative, glass half full way, for our suffering is not in vain. The Father is well aware of the seasons that He has called us to live in and will make them work out for our good (Romans 8:28). *"For it is better, if it is God's will, to suffer for doing good than for doing evil. "* 1 Peter 3:17 NIV.

I now realize that just by changing the angle at which we look at the moments of suffering, the mountains of despair can suddenly become climbable. Then we can let God begin to plant seeds of humility, gratefulness, and strength in place of the harmful counterproductive seeds we plant in our unstable emotional state. The spiritual seeds planted by the Father yield spiritual fruit that benefits us in this life and the next. When we are in right standing with the Lord and serving the kingdom of God, our suffering will be rewarded. *"But rejoice inasmuch as you participate in the sufferings of Christ, so that you may be overjoyed when his glory is revealed."* 1 Peter 4:13 NIV.

Therefore, my season of being a stay at home mom of five is where the Lord wants me to do my ministry right now. So I will do my best to serve my children in this season while remembering that any suffering that comes from this stage of life has its own rewards.

Whatever suffering we endure can be used as a testimony to bless others and that is a reward in itself.

Study Verse - 1 Peter 4:16 NIV

"However, if you suffer as a Christian, do not be ashamed, but praise God that you bear that name."

Dealing with Rejection

Rejection. An almost glossed over emotion. An emotion that every human has felt at some point in their life. A feeling that can leave lasting life changing effects on a person's total existence, even though most don't admit the feeling of rejected even exist within themselves, this feeling is robbing people of their joy every day. No one wants to feel rejected and they definitely don't want people to know they feel rejected. Most of us spend our lives trying to avoid this emotion, which can leave us either closed off and cold or wrapped up in a life of people pleasing. To better understand this issue, we are going to take a closer look.

Rejection: 1. the dismissal or refusing of a proposal, idea, etc. 2. the spurning of a person's affections.

Rejection is the result of a circumstance where you can either be accepted or refused by someone and they reject you and/or what you have to offer. Causing you to feel rejected.

Rejected: Dismissed as inadequate, inappropriate or not to one's taste.

Wow! Just reading the definitions hurt my feelings. This emotion, though very real, can cause some very make believe scenarios to play out in our minds. Often times when we feel rejected, we then jump to a conclusion about how that person feels about us. Causing an internal chain reaction of ill feelings. Many times those feelings are based solely on false scenario, assumption or presuppositions/pre-dispositions. We should really use those moments to reflect on how though we may feel temporarily rejected and unwanted by man, we have been chosen by the most high. We were handpicked by the King of Kings. Therefore, **any little rejection from a human on earth is already demolished by the acceptance we have from our Father**. We are chosen by Him daily and never rejected although some of us reject Him. *"You did not choose me, but I chose you and appointed you that you should go and bear fruit and that your fruit should abide….."* John 15:16 ESV. He chooses us.

Think long and hard about the last time you felt rejected. Where was the first place your mind went? Did you immediately feel defensive? Did you feel attacked? Or, did you just feel plain unwanted? The way we answer these questions reveals a lot about what we think of ourselves as well as the condition of our hearts. Our uncertainty about the worth we have to the Father will leave a gaping hole where security in Christ should be. Our defensive mindset reveals that we are in some way looking for a confirmation of some kind, from man that we don't need. Here is where dependence on manmade approval sneaks in and lays root where security in Jesus rightfully belongs. We have already been selected as first pick so any rejection by man thereafter is of little importance in the grand scheme of things.

Just like we talked about in Part 1, we cannot give a job to an unqualified candidate. People have no qualifications when it comes to making judgments and approval in regard to people who were created by the God of the universe. We are made eternally qualified through Christ Jesus. Though we may be rejected and disqualified by humans, there is no lasting merit of our worth in the decision of man to disqualify. Our worth is found in Christ and Christ alone. Not in relationships, not in jobs, not in us.

The residue of rejection can leave nasty messes to clean up and plenty of emotional damage so I don't expect this to be an overnight transition. Getting through the lasting effects of rejection can take years of counseling and thought re-training. Many people suffer from fear of commitment, loneliness, and other forms of life stalling patterns, thanks to one or more experiences with rejection. When we rely on the strength we have in our God and the confidence we have in His word, our choice to believe Him and not our feelings releases us from the grasp of fleshly response. Therefore, these experiences can become step stools rather than stumbling blocks.

Study Verse- Ephesians 1:4-5 ESV

"even as he chose us in him before the foundation of the world, that we should be holy and blameless before him. In love he predestined us for adoption as sons through Jesus Christ, according to the purpose of his will,"

Never Alone

We were created to be together. Together with each other and Him, collectively. The Father lovingly knit us together to as an extension of Him and in the likeness of Him and each other. No wonder, we long for companionship and connection. There is a longing inside of us to be together and have fulfillment through relationship. Our spirits crave affection and the warmth that can come from relationship. The lack thereof leaves us panting like a deer without water.
Leaving us to hold loneliness.

Loneliness is so painful, rather it be feeling physically alone or feeling internally alone. All of us have felt loneliness in one season of life or another. You know those wide-open spaces in life that leave us feeling destitute? When you feel completely deserted or misunderstood? When you feel invisible and mute because it just seems like no one can or wants to see you or hear you? Many times we have someone that may be there but we're still lonely. Lucky for us there is redemption even for our loneliness. We have a

Comforter and a Savior who is always there. He is ever present. *"The Lord himself goes before you and will be with you; he will never leave you nor forsake you. Do not be afraid; do not be discouraged."* Deuteronomy 31:8 NIV. We must resolve to tap into His present source by tapping in through prayer and activated faith. Our Father wants to be near us and engaged with us more than anyone we could long for here on earth. Our hearts long for His companionship.

Finding companionship and comfort in Christ means that you have a never ending well of comfort, joy, peace, and council. By no means does it mean that we will never feel lonely again but it does mean that we have a place to fill our cup when we are feeling empty. Though it's really hard to think about that source when you're feeling like you're feeling in that moment, practicing the art of praying your way out of loneliness could very well be your key to sanity, joy and peace. *"The Lord is far from the wicked, but he hears the prayer of the righteous."* Proverbs 15:29 NIV. He is always there, always listening and always waiting for us to run to Him. Remember that being alone is not a death sentence, it's just a season. All seasons change. Try to do your best to trust in the Lord in each season and you will be blessed.

The Lord is the master of all things including our life. He knows how long the seasons will last. Everything is His will and serves a purpose for our growth in Christ. *"give thanks in all circumstances; for this is God's will for you in Christ Jesus."* 1

Thessalonians 5:18 NIV. Loneliness is temporary but the love and deliverance of our Father is eternal.

Study Verse- 2 John 1:3 NIV

"Grace, mercy and peace from God the Father and from Jesus Christ, the Father's Son, will be with us in truth and love. "

Know That You Are Loved

For some reason, there is a misconception that Christians don't deal with the same emotional bondage that other people deal with. However, the fact stands that yes we are children of the Lord of Lords, but we are still in a struggle with the flesh. Struggling with insecurities and fighting against mental bondage that comes with our skin suit. Many of us are still struggling to believe that anyone would love us enough to die for us. Some of us are convinced that we are not loved or are unlovable. We get into our own heads and play with the lies of the enemy that try to convince us that there is nothing in us worth being loved. How can this be? He allowed men to beat Him, spit on Him, and ultimately kill Him for our sake. If that's not love I don't know what is. Jesus represents the epitome of love. He is love. Our Father gave up His only sinless child to save His heathen children who most of don't want anything to do with Him.

This life is hard so I can totally understand that you may have some guilt and shame. Who doesn't? Maybe you feel like God is absent or that He has taken something from you or that He has abandoned you. These are all lies of the enemy that keep us from experiencing God's love and freedom in its purest form. He will never leave or forsake you (Hebrews 13:5). That is why the Cross exists. To leave everything there. All the guilt, shame, sickness, embarrassment, hurt, and every other burden. *"But because of his great love for us, God, who is rich in mercy, made us alive with Christ even when we were dead in transgressions—it is by grace you have been saved."* Ephesians 2:4-5 NIV. His grace is sufficient for all that we let steal our joy. Our mistakes can never outweigh the love and grace we have been given by our Father. His love is unconditional and ours for the taking.

"Give thanks to the God of heaven. His love endures forever." Psalm 136:26 NIV. Though sometimes it may seem like no one cares about us, He loves us even when we don't love ourselves. His love will always be there no matter how far we drift and it is up to us to love Him enough to cling to Him. The love this world has to offer is based on circumstance but the love of the Lord is unconditional. You are loved by the one who holds the power of the universe. Who cares if your boss doesn't love you? Or, if your friend has turned against you? You have the attention of the creator. I'd say that is about as good as you can get and as loved as you can be.

Study Verse - Psalm 145:8 NIV

"The Lord is gracious and compassionate, slow to anger and rich in love."

Drawing From The Source

Source: a place, person, or thing from which something comes or can be obtained.

Our society has us fooled into believing that we are the producers of our own joy/happiness. In most instances, our world would have us to believe that if we just do what makes us feel good, we will be happy. The problem with this logic is that sort of happiness is very temporary and in most cases leaves us feeling just as empty or unhappy (sometimes more) as we were before and leaves us still in searching. Also, most things that our natural self wants, that makes us feel good and are sinful will lead us to eternal damnation rather than eternal joy. The flesh is naturally at odds with the Spirit of God. *"For the desires of the flesh are against the Spirit, and the desires of the Spirit are against the flesh, for these are opposed to each other, to keep you from doing the things you want to do. But if you are led by the Spirit, you are not under the law."* Galatians 5:17-18 ESV.

We are not equipped to produce the joy that our spirit longs for. Our brains can in no way calculate what it takes to satisfy the spirit. Mainly because we have not created ourselves. Only the Creator can know what satisfies us and what it takes to match our desire with true fulfillment. He knows our inner workings because He fashioned every part of us. *"For you formed my inward parts; you knitted me together in my mother's womb."* Psalm 139:13 ESV. With this truth, we can rest assure that the Father is our only source of satisfaction and we can trust that He knows what He's doing and what it takes to fulfill us. His Spirit will bring forth the joy that was created for us, in us.

Joy comes with several bits of evidence. We have different levels within our joy including, contentment, gladness, and cheerfulness. No matter how it manifests itself, true joy is produced only by the Holy Spirit (Galatians 5:22). The Spirit produces joy and we draw from the Spirit. This joy is holy and has no connection to situation or circumstance. It cannot be moved by the world because it is not of the world. It comes through faith (Romans 5:2). We cannot earn it through works and we cannot get it from any purchase at the mall. The standing of your heart's faith is the only thing that can bring true joy into your life.

It is up to us to choose to put our faith in our Lord and Savior and the Holy Spirit in to tap into the source of true joy. It is also up to us to detach ourselves from the worldly logic that is forced on us by our modern culture. Determining the difference between the world's joy and the joy of the Lord is key to finding the truth about happiness. Truthfully examine where you put your hope and faith. Do a course correction if necessary. Connect your heart with the source and indulge in the undeserved happiness offered to all who are righteous. Blessings!

Study Verse - Philippians 4:4 NLT

"Always be full of joy in the Lord. I say it again— rejoice!"

Joy In Spite Of....

It's so funny how sometimes when a friend tells us that something not so great has happened in their lives, we say things like, "Look on the bright side," "This too shall pass," or "Don't worry, it will all work out." However in the mist of our own catastrophe, the bright side is the last thing on our minds. And sometimes when someone quotes that line to us, we want to tell them where they can put their bright side, even though we know they are right. Think of all the times when you were in a terrible situation that that seemed to have no bright side and re-evaluate that situation. For instance, say you get in a car wreck that totals your new car. You feel like the world has ended. The bright side is, you are still alive and you have insurance. So what you will have to drive a rental or take the train to work for a while? At least you are alive to do both those things. Right?

It seems so easy to just see it in the proper light when we aren't in it. Unfortunately, our situation can bring so much fogginess to our right mindset. This is why it's vital to keep the truth in view so that it's easier to access when the fog begins to roll in.

The Word of God instructs us to be joyful always. *"Always be joyful."* 1 Thessalonians 5:16 NLT. That means no matter the situation or tragedy there is always a bright side. The Lord is always working in our favor no matter what it looks like around us. That is the most comforting feeling to have. To always know that though your life looks like its in shambles right now, if you have faith in your Lord and Savior, it will always work out for your victory and ultimate joy. *" Those who listen to instruction will prosper; those who trust the Lord will be joyful. "* Proverbs 16:20 NLT. As we look toward our Father and all that He has said and done, we can find comfort in knowing that He will take care of His children. *"As pressure and stress bear down on me, I find joy in your commands. "* Psalm 119:143 NLT. We can find joy in Him when times are looking bleak.

Remembering how far we've come and trusting where God is taking us serves as a light in what may seem like a locked dark room. A light that will help us to continue to see the call God has on our life. It is so hard to still serve and be obedient to the God's call when your life is in turmoil. You will find that when you serve no matter what, you will be blessed even more. *"Those who plant in tears will harvest with shouts of joy."* Psalm 126:5 NLT. Planting your ministry seed can be your seed of joy when you are serving with a joyful, thankful heart. We must remember that there is always something to be thankful for. We have been saved from the grips of death and that is by far enough to be grateful and joyful for. Look at the "bright side," it's always there.

"Taste and see that the Lord is good. Oh, the joys of those who take refuge in him!" Psalm 34:8 NLT

Recognizing My Blessings

Sometimes in the midst of a storm, we get side tracked and forget about all the things God has done and still is doing in our life. We get so caught up in the situation that we can only focus on what seems to be the major thing happening. We do this failing to realize that we have so much to be thankful for that is also happening. Somehow we forget about the air we breathe and food on the table. If we were in a third world country, food would be like a sack of gold and we would think we just won the lottery. *"Be thankful in all circumstances, for this is God's will for you who belong to Christ Jesus."* 1 Thessalonians 5:18 NLT. Being human our minds sometimes can be consumed with the flesh world and we forget about the spiritual realm where the true reality is. Looking beyond our circumstance and seeing that we have so much to be grateful for is necessary to keeping our sanity, and strengthening our faith during those hard times. *"Give thanks to the Lord, for he is good! His faithful love endures forever."* Psalm 136:1 NLT. No matter what we are going through, the love of our Father never changes. When we are suffering He is right there with us.

162

The Bible instructs us to be thankful and give God praise. *"Give thanks to the Lord and proclaim his greatness. Let the whole world know what he has done."* 1 Chronicles 16:8 NLT. People who are thankful for what they have are happier because they are content with not having more. Being grateful for what you have will also keep you from constantly wanting more. In a world consumed by a deluge of ungratefulness and want, choosing to be grateful is like speaking a foreign language. This is why our nation's debt is out of control. Enough is never enough and good enough won't do. The sin of mankind created a black hole of want in the flesh, and our spirit man cries out for a spiritual need that can only be fulfilled by Christ Jesus. Our grateful heart reveals humility and honors God by praising Him for what He has already done and who He is helps to adjust our thinking so that our worship comes before our want. Giving praise to the Lord is like a sweet fragrance to Him. He lavishes in our praise. We can praise him in many ways. We can dance, we can sing, and we can praise Him through how we live our lives. *"Let everything that breathes sing praises to the Lord! Praise the Lord!"* Psalm 150:6 NLT. Be grateful and be blessed!

Study Verse - Psalm 68:19 NLT

"Praise the Lord; praise God our savior! For each day he carries us in his arms."

CHOICE CHALLENGE #6:

Making the Choice to See the Glass Full

"We can complain because rose bushes have thorns or rejoice because thorn bushes have roses." -Abraham Lincoln

For me, on the battlefield of motherhood, it can be hard to see the roses when it seems like you have better chances of seeing soiled linen. Your eyes can be so full of dirty dishwater that you can't see the win. The same goes for any other season of life. The circumstances around us can seem so overtaking that they stand between us and hope and leaving us grasping in the dark even without hope for the light. *"Hope deferred makes the heart sick, but a dream fulfilled is a tree of life."* Proverbs 13:12. It takes a consistent hope to fuel the plucky optimism we need to see the bright side. Thank God we have it in Jesus.

This brings us to our next choice challenge, "Making the choice to see the glass full." Seeing the glass half full isn't quite full enough. Seeing the glass full is knowing where our hope is and seeing the good in the midst of the circumstance. The good in every circumstance is the God in every circumstance. He is in every season and every circumstance. It's up to us to make the choice to see Him. Our FULL glass is Jesus.

He is the hope in the trial, the light in the dark and the rose in the thorn bush.

"This is why we work hard and continue to struggle, for our hope is in the living God, who is the Savior of all people and particularly of all believers." 1 Timothy 4:10. Fixing our eyes on the true hope will change our perspective and adjust our focus so that we can move forward with a victorious mindset and a joyful heart. We already have the victory no matter what it looks like around us. So today let's look at the roses. Let's find Jesus in every space. Let's look at the glass full!

Today, let's sit and think of the season we are in. Then, let's think about how the hope we have in Jesus changes how we see where we are. Take time to write out the full glass perspective of where you are in life right now and ask God to help you to keep that right perspective.

"Rejoice in our confident hope. Be patient in trouble, and keep on praying." Romans 12:12

Prayer:

Lord Jesus, thank You for the hope I have in You. Please help me to see You in all seasons of life. Lord help me to have a full glass perspective as I see things through Your eyes. Remove the deception that keeps me from seeing Your truth. I surrender my reactions, reasoning, and rights to You. In Jesus name, Amen!

My Journey

What areas have allowed complaint to steal my joy?

Where am I allowing self-pity to gain headway?

How can I better my response to negative outcomes?

What have I allowed to stand between me and hope?

Discussion Questions

What did I learn about myself in this section?

What Scriptures stood out to me in this section?

What life application do I intend to implement with the discoveries that I have made?

Journaling Page

Part 7

Offer What You Have Been Given

I don't know about you, but I love free stuff. I love offers that come no strings attached. I get all excited when free trials come in the mail with no fine print and I kind of feel like I've gotten over on the company who gave the offer because usually I have no intention of buying their product ever. You know what I mean, and in you're mind you're thinking, "ah-ha! Suckers! I am not buying your product! But, thanks for the free stuff!"

Often this is how we treat what we have been offered and given by Christ. We're like "Thanks for the free stuff, but I'm not buying the product." We have been given overflowing mercy and grace in forgiveness that exceeds human comprehension and yet we take it for ourselves and refuse to invest it in others. Our self-righteousness would have us to believe that we are worth forgiving, but that maybe others aren't quite worth our investment in forgiveness and grace. Little do we know, that the joy we are looking for is wrapped up in our obedient investment in forgiveness and grace.

Christ's gift of forgiveness and grace is free to us, but He also calls us to "buy" the product and offer it to others. Our faith is best walked out when we walk in the footsteps that have already been walked by Jesus. In those footsteps we walk out what He has given us by giving it to others. This leads us on to our next topic.

Remember That You Are Forgiven

The human brain is a funny thing. As quickly as we see or hear or learn something, we can quickly forget it. We hear a phone number recited to us and if we aren't repeating it back or making a photographic note in our memory, we immediately forget most of the digits. Most of us have to take notes in order to remember things of importance with accuracy. The brain has a way of filtering out specific things. For some reason it seems that we frequently "filter out" the things that have been done for us and hang on quite tightly to the things that have not been done for us or things that were unpleasantly done to us by another. Someone can bless us with a meal on Monday and in that moment we express adoring gratitude. But, don't let them offend us on Friday, because every nice thing they have ever done is suddenly erased and forgotten while we harp on the two-minute event that "hurt our feelings." Though this sounds ridiculous when we put it on paper, this is a reality of how we behave from time to time.

Our offense meters weigh in and we decide who deserves grace or not. How do we come to the conclusion that we have a right to gauge who deserves grace? How can we make decisions about something we have not made available? Who put us in charge of the grace rations? Why do we forget that we have received grace not of our own ability but by the generosity of the Father?

Our forgetfulness leaves others at the mercy of our justified anger and willingness to extend grace leaves us in a cloud of pride and un-forgiveness. I'd say that it might be a good idea to take notes that will remind us of what we have been given. Though it seems like it would be easy to remember the fact that we were destined for death and damnation and were snatched out of the grips of hell, would make it a little easier for us to recall the facts about our salvation. Somewhere along the way we lose touch with what salvation means, and how we received it because of the sacrifice made on our behalf. Not because of any works that we have done. We received that salvation for free. Though there is a cost to follow Jesus, we have not paid any price for the grace, forgiveness and salvation that we have received. How do we conclude that others have to earn it from us when we have received it based on the merit of another?

"For God so loved the world, that He gave His only Son, that whoever believes in Him should not perish but have eternal life." John 3:16 ESV

The grace that we receive and the grace that we give, has been bought with the life of Christ. His blood has swung the door of grace wide open. We should not be an obstruction to the flow.

Maybe it's our own selves that we are having a hard time offering grace. Maybe you are like I was for years, and just can't seem to shake the shame and guilt that haunts you in the night, keeping you in a state of self-condemnation and you just can't forgive yourself for what you have done in your past. You keep getting close to the line but just can't seem to cross over to the freedom that lives in forgiveness. I have hung out in this space in different stages of life and it's never gratifying or redeeming in the least. This is where the enemy wants us to hang out so that we can never experience the gifts that the Father has for us. Because if we focus on us and what we have done, we can't see Jesus and what He's done.

It's vital to remember that we have been forgiven and lavished upon with grace. That we have been pardoned and paid for. We have to remember this truth because when we remember what has been done for us and the manner in which it was done (without any effort on our part) we can freely give of the same gift to without expecting something in return.

Let the Past Stay in the Past

Like a ball and chain our past can drag us down and make us slow to progress. Finding joy can be a hard search if you are always looking backward to see what happened in the years before. Could you image watching an Olympic runner headed to the finish line looking backwards? He would not be able to run as fast, keep his balance, watch for obstacles, or focus very well. Odds are that he would not win the race and would most likely get injured before he made it anywhere near the finish line. All of his hard work preparing for this race would have been wasted. I assume that the runner would be filled with regret and grief over his now lost Olympic career all because he could not focus on the goal, but kept looking at the trail behind him.

Our past can ruin our future if we let it. When looking at the things that have happened in our lives, there are two ways to go. We can either go in a direction that will show growth from the past or we can go in the direction that shows that we are still living in the past. A prime example of this is the **un-forgiveness** we addressed in the previous section. Holding on to a bad situation and being angry with someone who has hurt you in the past is like putting those cement shoes back on. You are not going very far and you hinder your own relationship with God. You have unconsciously given that person control over you and your emotions. Your unforgiving harms you more than the person you are upset with as well as stops your blessings from freely flowing. We must remember, *"But if you do not forgive others their sins, your Father will not forgive your sins."* Matthew 6:15NIV. If God has shown us such mercy, who are we to withhold it from our fellow man?

Another reoccurring issue of the past is regret for mistakes that we may have made. This is an issue for a large majority of people who have yet to find true happiness. The truth of the matter is that, if not for our mistakes, we would not learn and if not for learning we would not be refined. We must trust that everything that has happened in our lives is a part of God's divine plan. We were not made to understand His will, just to follow it. Our past can be a great working testimony. It could minister to many. We all have a story and someone needs your story for encouragement. Your life, any part of it, was not a mistake, but a miraculous unfolding of destiny.

Study Verse - Isaiah 43:18 NIV

"Forget the former things; do not dwell on the past."

CHOICE CHALLENGE #7:

Making the Choice to Give More Grace

"Making the Choice to Give MORE GRACE". Today we are going to be incredibly generous with the grace that we dish out. We are going to remember all that has been forgiven and covered by our Redeemer and offer that same favor to those around us. After all, it's pretty clear in His word that there are consequences for choosing to deny grace. *"For if you forgive others their trespasses, your heavenly Father will also forgive you, but if you do not forgive others their trespasses, neither will your Father forgive your trespasses."* Matthew 6:14-15 ESV.

It's really simple if we think of God's main concern, "Love your neighbor as yourself." If we put that to use intentionally, paired with a humble heart, it will make it easier to give grace generously. We all need grace and we all want for people to extend it where we fail. It should be a constant cycle among us like a pulley system. We must each reside on either end transferring the grace from one to another. However, the pulley system only works properly with humility as the rope. *"Always be humble and gentle. Be patient with each other, making allowance for each other's faults because of your love. Make every effort to keep yourselves united in the Spirit, binding yourselves together with peace."* Ephesians 4:2-3 NLT.

Prayer:

Lord Jesus, today I thank You for the grace and mercy that You have shown to me. Give me Your heart so that I can generously give the grace that You have given to me to share. I bind every spirit of pride that would hinder me from forgiving and freely giving mercy. Strengthen me in humility and bind the tongue that would hinder Your will. Thank You, God for Your work in me. In Jesus name, Amen!

My Journey

What areas have I had a hard time extending grace?

What areas have I had a hard time receiving grace?

What circumstances have I allowed to limit my generosity with grace?

Who have I held un-forgiveness in my heart for?

Where have I allowed bitterness to creep in?

What past struggle have I allowed to take up space in my present?

Discussion Questions

What did I learn about myself in this section?

What Scriptures stood out to me in this section?

What life application do I intend to implement with the discoveries that I have made?

Journaling Page

_____

_____

_____

_____

_____

_____

_____

_____

_____

_____

_____

_____

_____

_____

_____

_____

_____

_____

_____

_____

_____

_____

_____

_____

Part 8

Believing God

If He Can Do That....

Why do we question God? Why do we weigh Him on scales to try and measure Him up? Why is it that no matter how much He has shown us, we insist on holding back our full trust in Him? Our flesh is why! Our flesh is prideful, selfish, rebellious and noncompliant. No wonder it's vital that our flesh be wrangled into submission by our spirit man. It's never satisfied and, therefore, needs to be quenched again and again.

During my prayer time recently, I have been convicted of not giving God enough credit. You know what I mean. When we pray with the "kinda" faith. As if we know His limitations (which there are none) or something. So, we send our prayer to Him with a lasso on it just in case we need to pull it back and handle it ourselves. Or, when praying for things that we think are possible, instead of knowing that we serve a God who can do the impossible. I had been praying for things and forgetting that I was praying to the all mighty, omnipotent and eternal God. Thus putting a ceiling on some of my requests. I had been limiting my blessings and the magnitude of the work that He can do in my life by not remembering the power and unlimited abilities that our God possesses.

Lets take a look at His track record. In Genesis 1:1, *"In the beginning, God created the heavens and the earth."*, He fed 4000 people with only five loaves of bread and a couple fish (Matthew 15:32-39), He spoke to Moses through a burning bush (Exodus 3), and so many more things that need no mention, because among all of these incredible doings, Jesus, the second part of the trinity of God, raised himself from the dead. Need I say more!

I make mention of all this because for some reason, we seem to forget all that He can do when we think of all that we need. We seem to think we can out imagine, out problem solve and out think God. Forgetting that His thoughts and ways are not our thoughts or ways (Isaiah 55:8). Which brings up a very important question.....

Do You Really Believe He Is Who He says He Is?

Now, don't answer that question too quickly. Really think about it. Ask yourself "how much credit have I given Him?" Have you been simply underestimating Him or is there a serious belief issue that you may be dealing with? It's very important to think about this because our salvation depends on the genuineness of our faith in Christ. Many people claim that they believe in God and/or Jesus, but it is very clear that if you look closely at the life displayed, the biblical definition of belief in Him is not being portrayed. The truth of the matter is that if we don't believe that God is who He says He is, then we cannot truly believe in what He can do either. Our faith should be connected with trust in His word. Our trust in His word means that we trust Him even when it doesn't make logical human sense. Our human sense becomes secondary to the God sense revealed to us through Scripture.

Scripture gives us a very clear picture of who God is. So if we have a wavering belief, it is on our end. God reveals Himself to us with consistency and clarity. In Scripture we are shown the Father's characteristics and His intent. He loves us (John 3:15-16), He is eternal (Deut. 33:27), He is a God of faithfulness (Deut. 32:4), He is trustworthy (Psalms 93:5), He is Holy (Isaiah 6:3, Rev. 4:8), He is just (Deut. 32:4, Rev. 15:3), He is full of grace (John 1:14), He is merciful (Deut. 4:31, Psalms 103:8), He is powerful (Psalms 147:5), He's a healer (Psalms 147:3; 103:3), and He is ABLE (Matt. 19:26)! Just to name a few. How can we doubt Him if we trust

183

in these truths? When we know Him well through His word, it's easier to trust and believe Him. Our relationship with the Father needs the same nurturing and attention as the relationships we cherish here on earth. A true relationship is based on quality time spent, communication and trust. Our quality time spent engaging in the word, our communication through prayer and the trust we develop through those practices brings us into a loving Father child relationship where we can be sure that our Father can be trusted at His word.

Let us not allow our human mental limitations to hinder our relationship with Christ, our prayer life or our ability to believe and do more. Remember the God we serve and that all things are possible through Him (Phillipians 4:13). Remember that His has no limits. Staying connected to His word will nurture our faith and belief in His abilities and attributes.

Study Verse - 1 John 5:14-15

"And this is the confidence that we have toward him, that if we ask anything according to his will he hears us. And if we know that he hears us in whatever we ask, we know that we have the requests that we have asked of him."

Know How Powerful Our God Is

Our little minds cannot possibly imagine what God is capable of. His power exceeds the human imagination. He just has to speak and anything can happen. "And God said, *"Let there be light,"* and there *was light."* Genesis 1:3 NIV. The most amazing part of it all is that He is on our side. Our only job is to have faith in Him and trust in His power. If we step back and really take in all that depends on the hand of the Lord (everything), our brains just cannot comprehend it all. His power governs our life. The air we breathe is literally one word of God away from depletion. What a sobering thought. Nothing can happen beyond His might and He has authority over all.

There are so many instances in the Bible where God displayed His power. Too many to list all of them but let's look at just one. Remember the parting of the sea (Exodus 14:21-31)? Can you part a sea? I'm sure that's not in my skill set. I don't think even the greatest magician could pull that one off. Could you imagine standing at the shore of the sea at that very moment? What were the faces of the Hebrews like? They were probably so stunned that they forgot what they were doing for a second. They stood before one of the greatest miracles recorded in the Bible. And yet still they questioned the almighty God.

After reading that, I'm sure you kind of shake your head like I do when I think about the fact that the Hebrews totally devalued God's incredible power shortly after bearing witness of His greatness. But you know what? We do the same thing all the time. We completely forget how much He has done even in our own lives. What if we remained in awe of what He has done and can do? What if we thought to ourselves "If God can part a sea, what could He do with my issue?" Our little issues that we think are so major can be fixed by a single word. *"The voice of the Lord is powerful; the voice of the Lord is majestic."* Psalm 29:4 NIV. If we have no faith in the power of God, it can't do us any good. We must stand before our Red Sea and just believe in His power while we watch Him move the water.

His power in our lives is only limited by our faith.

With little faith, we will see seemingly little power. With big faith, we can see His true unlimited power. He gives us power through our faith. If we believe in Him, He will give us power to do things we thought were impossible. Our obstacle can be that we are so busy looking at what we think can or will happen, that we forget who has control of it all. How confused we can be. Our God's power is not limited by the boundaries of this world and the things we see. *"For we live by faith, not by sight."* Corinthians 5:7 NIV.

Knowing that our Father, who has our best interest in mind, controls the universe is more than enough reason to be joyful and sing His praises. When the storm rolls in to steal your joy, *"Proclaim the power of God, whose majesty is over Israel, whose power is in the heavens."* Psalm 68:34 NIV. Always remember His power.

Study Verse - 1 Corinthians 6:14 NIV

"By his power God raised the Lord from the dead, and he will raise us also."

It's OK to Have No Control

I know someone reading this just had a mini panic attack at the mere thought of not being in control. And, that's OK. Take a couple deep cleansing breaths and hop back in with me.

I completely understand those insane thoughts that tell you it's a necessity to be in control of one scenario or another, one person or another, or possibly all. Trust me, we are walking this out together. Especially when you read text in the Bible that says things like, *"We may throw the dice, but the Lord determines how they fall."* Proverbs 16:33 NLT. Then your heart starts pounding a little like your running a 5K but then you get a grip and realize who God is. You might even think to yourself, "OK God I trust you!" but soon after you start thinking strategically about how you are going to throw the dice to land in your favor. You know just plain, certifiable thoughts. I am totally with you on this. Praise God for His unfailing grace and patience with us.

We work so hard to get control over our lives to make things go the way we have "planned". When in actuality, we have no control over anything and waste a great amount of unnecessary emotion and energy on situations where we have made no effort to consult God in the matter. Then it comes time for things to happen and they fall apart. All those spread sheets and lists cannot replace God's will or wisdom. When we are actively working under God's will, things go smoother and, in most cases, the end result is a lot better than you expected.

Wouldn't it be great if life had less roadblocks and you felt less stress trying to figure life out? Well I have news for you, we may not be able to remove the roadblocks in life but we can leave the concern for them to the professional. All we have to do is stop operating on our own clock and start operating on God's time instead. We need to pray and ask the Father for guidance in our lives rather than giving Him a list of our intentions and desires and before we make life-altering decisions, we can act in accordance with God's plans and rest in His peace along the way. We can't just wait until our plans fall through to pray for help. Consulting the Lord before making decisions is a great way to keep our future in the right hands. Not our own. We can be sure to see an incredible success rate of improvement as well as a sanity increase when we operate in God's will.

"Study this Book of Instruction continually. Meditate on it day and night so you will be sure to obey everything written in it. Only then will you prosper and succeed in all you do." Joshua 1:8 NLT

When we chose to be obedient rather than in control, we chose to cultivate success, eternal wealth, and joy. Things we all want. Operating in the will of God can only result in a blessed and righteous life. Letting the Lord take control alleviates us from the stress of trying to make things happen because our Father is already in control.

In your journal, write down areas in your life where you need to let God come in and take control. Be truthful with yourself so that you can release those areas to the Lord. Pray for the Lord to come in and take control and that He helps you to let go. Have faith that your Father has your best interest at heart. Record your prayer in your journal and pray it often.

CHOICE CHALLENGE #8:

Making the Choice to Believe God

"Making the Choice to Believe God" seems really simple actually. Most Christians would say, "of course I believe God". While this might seem like a pointless challenge for us to venture on, let's take a few minutes to think about how much of our belief is really belief. We can read Scripture and recite it and even let the world know how much we believe the words we have read, but in many separate areas we may be lacking a true trust in God's word. For instance, we may say that we believe that God will give us peace, but we may not be reaching to Him to get it. Or we may say we believe that God will provide for us, but are scared to pay our tithes for fear that we won't make rent. Let's just keep it real. It's easy to say it and proclaim it but the actual action of truly believing and trusting His Word takes a little extra step of faith.

"Trust in the Lord with all your heart ; do not depend on your own understanding. " Proverbs 3:5NLT. The "own understanding" is what messes us up in the whole trust situation. This is where the doubt, control and faith thieves come in. Our own understanding causes us to use human logic to figure things out. It causes us to only believe a little instead of fully. Trusting in the Lord goes beyond human logic because He has completely different logic. *"'My thoughts are nothing like your thoughts,' says the Lord. 'And my*

ways are far beyond anything you could imagine.' " Isaiah 55:8 NLT. We have to get to a place where we believe God and His word even when it doesn't make any logical sense to us. It's our job to stand on the His word. We can fully believe Him and trust that He will see His promises through because our God is not untrustworthy. *"Remember that Christ came as a servant to the Jews to show that God is true to the promises he made to their ancestors."* Romans 15:8 NLT

The Lord's words are true and unshakable *("Make them Holy by your truth; teach them your Word which is truth."* John 17:17 NLT). Which gives us stable ground to stand on and build on. We can believe in Him but most importantly today, we can BELIEVE HIM. He speaks truth to us and over us. When we walk closely with Him daily it becomes easier to take Him at His word. Get close to the Father! He's waiting.

Prayer:

Lord, thank You for Your truths. Thank You for Your patience as we figure this trust thing out. Help us Lord to release our own understanding to You so that we can believe You and Your Word. Woo us to come close to You and rest on Your Word. Thank You, God for Your endless grace. In Jesus Name, AMEN!!!

My Journey

Where have I struggled to believe God?

How have I held back in my prayer life?

What attributes of the Father have I struggled to believe and trust?

What areas have I trusted in my power over the power of God?

What areas have I tried to hold on to control? What has been the impact?

Discussion Questions

What did I learn about myself in this section?

What Scriptures stood out to me in this section?

What life application do I intend to implement with the discoveries that I have made?

Journaling Page

_____

_____

_____

_____

_____

_____

_____

_____

_____

_____

_____

_____

_____

_____

_____

_____

_____

_____

_____

_____

_____

_____

Part 9

Be Iron

Hopefully you have been able to practice putting firm belief in God's word since the last section. I've learned that believing God's word offers freedom in our everyday lives that can't be captured anywhere else. Even though I try consistently to make a conscious effort to believe the words of the Father, I notice that there are some moments that are a little harder for me to lean on that belief. So I choose to focus on really putting that belief into action and I immensely enjoy letting go. Learning to believe God's word will be a great tool for us as we walk into the next part of our journey together.

Looking at the title of this chapter you may be perplexed and think, "Why are we talking about iron?" Let me assure you that we are still headed in our same direction toward Christ's lasting joy. Somewhere along the line, we underestimated how much God does through others for us and through us for others in the building of His Kingdom. In this section, we will talk about what that looks like practically and how some adjustments in our thought process can make a big difference in our footprint on our path to joy.

LIFE and The Value of Selflessness

OK, so now that we've dealt with some hard stuff, let's take a more external route in our journey.

If you've been around for a good number of years, you've likely heard the name Mother Theresa. Mother Theresa was a phenomenal patriarch and model of disciplined selflessness. So much so that her name is known around the world for her good deeds and willingness to serve others. She left a legacy of service and obedience to God. The world has several lights shining like Mother Theresa, people who live outside of themselves on purpose and in obedience. All of us have it in us, but it can be a struggle for some of us to bring it to the surface. The greater part of the human population has lived with a healthy helping of selfserving thoughts and selfish characteristics. Some of these characteristics have even been disguised in philanthropic or giving acts.

Selfish: having or showing concern only for yourself and not for the needs or feelings of other people.

Most of us don't realize how selfish we can be. Many of us have also not connected the dots that selfishness and pride are at the base of most evil/sinful actions we partake in. Our personal wants and desires can lead us down a path of destruction, justification and false beliefs. A good portion of sin stems from our need to be satisfied for one reason or another. Infidelity occurs when one spouse's selfish desires outweighs the importance of the other spouse's needs to them. People are envious when they want something so bad that someone else has it makes them upset, unhappy or even hateful to the point of action.

The flesh wants to be satisfied through all of our senses. We want to be entertained through our eyes and ears and things have to taste good and feel good and we often conclude that whatever feels good is what we should do. How unfortunate for the human race. If selfishness were the key to happiness we would have it all figured out. The truth is….selfishness is the enemy of happiness. Granted, a good portion of people don't deal with selfishness on an extreme level but it can be a slow fade to a self-centered existence with all that comes with it. For the more extreme cases, the consequences are more obvious. They usually affect the people around you first and then you at a deeper level and can lead to isolation, depression, loneliness, excessive anger and other narcissistic behavior.

In the culture we live in today, many of our lives have become self-indulging, monotonous or meaningless and survival-driven. We have become survivors for the most part, instead of people who live and have life. I am sure that when Jesus died on the cross, His motivation was not for us to be able to spend

197

more time at the office. I'm sure He was also not trying to give us the opportunity to have "one last drink" or a couple more opportunities for fornication. He came so that we could live! *"The thief comes only to steal and kill and destroy. I came that they may have life and have it abundantly."* John 10:10 ESV

So what are we doing? Why have we decided to take the world's "normal" road and not the road of life? Trading happiness for the hamster wheel life? Because living a lifestyle offered by the world we live in has nothing to offer except for the hamster wheel effect. When you're steadily running on this wheel of sin and self- gratification, then you keep circling around to the same unhappy truth: lack of fulfillment, depression, bitterness, guilt, shame, un-forgiveness and a life that cannot be blessed, due to the chosen circumstance. The Christian life was never intended to be a life of consumption but a life if constant outpour. *"Do nothing out of selfish ambition or vain conceit. Rather, in humility value others above yourselves,"* Philippians 2:3 NIV. Being Christ like is by definition being selfless. Our wants and needs are well known by our Father and we are His priority. So there is no need to be consumed with selfishness or to revert to survival mode. *"Don't be concerned for your own good but for the good of others. "* 1 Corinthians 10:24 NLT.

Here's a look at the less destructive, alternative route. The blessed route. Romans 12:1-2 NLT *(*also read the ESV translation*) "Therefore, I urge you, brothers and sisters, in view of God's mercy, to offer your bodies as a living sacrifice, holy and pleasing to God – this is* *your true and proper worship. Do not conform to the pattern of this world, but be transformed by the renewing of your mind. Then you will be able to test and approve what God's will is – His good, pleasing and perfect will."* The key to living a joyful blessed life is allowing God to transform your mind, adjust your thinking and pour in His will for you. Our thoughts create a world for us. Conquering our worldly thoughts and replacing them with God's truth will jumpstart the outward life change.

The Holy Spirit is the cure for the common human. *"The acts of the flesh are obvious: sexual immorality, impurity and debauchery; idolatry and witchcraft; hatred, discord, jealousy, fits of rage, selfish ambition, dissensions, factions and envy; drunkenness, orgies, and the like. I warn you, as I did before, that those who live like this will not inherit the kingdom of God."* Galatians 5:19-21 NIV. All of the above are flesh driven and self-focused. The Holy Spirit teaches us to live a life of righteousness leading to peace and joy. *"But the fruit of the Spirit is love, joy, peace, forbearance, kindness, goodness, faithfulness, gentleness and self-control. Against such things there is no law."* Galatians 5:22-23 NIV.

Our lives are meant to be full of love, joy and peace. Not accounting, schedules and phone calls. It is so easy to become submerged in what our world considers living: money, possessions and self-gratification. However, the truth is that those things could bring the opposite of life and living a life in survival mode is a life lived in vain. *"Riches won't help on the Day of*

Judgment, but right living can save you from death." Proverbs 11:4.

Though sometimes it may seem hard to release our hold on our personal desires and what may seem like such important things to us, the blessing is in the giving not the receiving. In the giving of love, the giving of time, the giving of self, and many other things, we find what we're really after. I challenge you to put your precious desires second (while the Father cares for them) and be blessed by putting someone else in first place for a change. I challenge all of us to take a step back and honestly evaluate our current priorities. Is your life a little too parallel to what today's culture has approved? Have your thoughts given way to what the world says you are? Do some self-investigating and get honest with yourself and God. Write down the changes you feel you may need to make in order to transition from a "hamster wheel" existence, to a LIFE. Get in God's word and find the truth about what real life should be. We were meant for so much more.

Study Verses - John 10:10

"The thief's purpose is to steal and kill and destroy. My purpose is to give them a rich and satisfying life."

Galatians 5:16-17 ESV

"But I say, walk by the Spirit, and you will not gratify desires of the flesh. For the desires of the Spirit are against the flesh, for those are opposite to each other, to keep you from doing the things you want to do."

We All Need Sharpening

Sometimes in life some of us get a tad bit confused and come to a conclusion that we are pretty well off in knowledge and start to believe that we can only be corrected or rebuked or taught by certain people. Many of us have a reserved section in our mind for the people who are allowed to speak into our lives. Then strategically close off others who may have been called to drop a nugget of wisdom on us. This is pride working overtime in this scenario. Although it may not seem to be on a large scale, it may be wreaking havoc in areas that aren't so easy to spot in your life. Pride wants us to believe that we are the sharp one whom sharpens others but we need no sharpening.

"As iron sharpens iron, so one person sharpens another." Proverbs 27:17 NIV

The act of blade sharpening requires a rubbing together of two counterparts. Both parts are of equal importance. Both parts are very necessary for the process. A knife could not possibly sharpen itself. As interesting as that visual might be, it's just not possible. Likewise, we cannot become sharp and useful without the necessary counterparts.

We were not put on this earth to try and learn what we deemed necessary and then go about our business.

Other people being around us, is not just for our entertainment. We are commissioned to help one another draw wisdom from each other and grow together. Think of good friends as iron knives and every time we come in contact with each other in a mentally stimulating event, we glide blades (our minds and inner self), which make our blades sharper, if we allow them to. Not to say that everyone in our life should be able to guide us, however, we should be able to learn from our interactions, even if we are just using that friend's life as a learning experience of what not to do. Many times the Lord will use a very unlikely source to bring forth wisdom but we may not receive it because of the packaging. Allowing people close to us to sharpen us allows us to become wiser, stronger, inspired, aware, and the list goes on.

Collaborating with a good friend helps us to make better choices and filter out the bad choices. Every person in our lives drops a little something in our basket as we go through life. It is up to us if and how we use it. We are always in need of growing and becoming wiser. These things never cease to have value. *"How much better to get wisdom than gold! To get understanding is to be chosen rather than silver."* Proverbs 16:16. If we think we have it all figured out already, it just shows we still have a long way to go. The ego is our worst enemy when it comes to our growth. Pride will tell you that you have already "arrived," and by default keep you stagnant. In contrast, humility will allow the doors of growth to be open to wisdom and understanding. We must deflate one to enlarge the other.

Study Verse - Job 34:4 NIV

"Let us discern for ourselves what is right; let us learn together what is good."

Be Hungry for Wisdom

Wisdom: 1. The ability to discern or judge what is true, right, or lasting; insight. 2. Common sense; good judgment. 3. Knowledge. 4. A wise outlook, plan, or course of action.

Sofia (Wisdom in Greek): wisdom, learning, sapience, sage-ness

It's no wonder that the Bible mentions how important gaining wisdom is. I will point out though, that this definition also includes "common sense", and I have noticed in life that common sense is just not as "common" as it would seem. But, we'll let God deal with that....moving on!

"Wisdom is more valuable than gold and crystal. It cannot be purchased with jewels mounted in fine gold." Job 28:17 NLT. God's people need wisdom to navigate through life. Wisdom and proper counsel will keep us from falling into the traps and dangers of our world and of our flesh that keep us in dark places.

The problem for most of us, though, is that we are so caught up with trying to hear, watch, and read the latest thing that our brains are low on space for the knowledge that we really need to absorb and retain. If we could just replace an hour of our day that we use for useless information with an hour to read the Bible, listen to a sermon or just spend time in meditation and actually digest what we learn or receive, we would probably escape the many unproductive, misdirected situations that we get into. However, we have to be willing to make wisdom a priority.

The book of Proverbs makes plenty mention of wisdom. Not just any wisdom, true wisdom that comes from the Lord (James 3:14:18). Why? Because, wisdom can keep us from making mistakes, getting involved with the wrong people, as well as helping us to advise others looking for wise counsel. *"Wisdom will save you from evil people, from those whose words are twisted."* Proverbs 2:12 NLT. Foolish people walk into the traps set for them even if they can see it coming but wise people can sense something bad coming and veer away from it. Wisdom is a knife that requires sharpening, reading the Word and seeking wise counsel sharpens the sword of wisdom. Many people underestimate the power of wisdom and instead try to replace it with money. Money without wisdom is like dust in a vent with no filter. If you don't know how to be a good steward of that money, it will pass right through your fingers and will it not be a blessing. If you are wise and are faithful with the finances that you have been given instead of depending on it, it can be a blessing to you instead of a curse. There is no tangible replacement for wisdom.

God is the professor who teaches us discernment and gives us His wisdom. Seeking Him will lead to discernment through the Holy Spirit and unsurpassed wisdom. *"In him lie hidden all the treasures of wisdom and knowledge."* Colossians 2:3 NLT. Our flesh wants us to think that we can figure things out on our own, even though most of our lifetime lines have proven that in fact we aren't the wisest beings when we try to take control. If it wasn't for the mercy and grace of the Lord, we would barely exist. We can barely figure out how to pay the bills let alone try to figure out what should happen next in our lives. I can barely remember my kids' names half the time or how to get from point A to B. So I'm sure that I would be totally spastic without God's loving guidance in all areas of my life. *"No human wisdom or understanding or plan can stand against the Lord."* Proverbs 21:30 NLT. We need His wisdom, direction and love to guide us and quiet our flesh. When we follow His direction we uncover a joy we could have never found on our own, the joy that comes with the peace of God's understanding.

Study Verse - Proverbs 2:6 NLT

"For the Lord grants wisdom! From his mouth come knowledge and understanding."

Being a Doer...

The Word of God is a powerful thing and it can really change your life, if you let it. I'm sure you've noticed that I like the phrase "if you let it". Here's why. Our choices and responses can either open or close doors of God-portunities to us. Oh, you're wondering what that word means? God-portunities is "God opportunities". We can easily shut ourselves out of great chances to exercise faith and grow by simply opting out. We can read the Word every day, all day and memorize many Scriptures, but if we are not living the word, it is all in vain. The Bible is not just intended to be a book of good stories and miracles. It is a book of instruction intended to guide us.

"Study this Book of Instruction continually. Meditate on it day and night so you will be sure to obey everything written in it. Only then will you prosper and succeed in all you do." Joshua 1:8 (NLT).

"All Scripture is breathed out by God and profitable for teaching, for reproof, for correction, and for training in righteousness, that the man of God may be complete, equipped for every good work." 2 Timothy 3:16-17

Reading the Word can only do so much without the action. We were chosen as children and disciples for Christ. Yes, because we are loved and He wants us to have eternal live, but also to take action against the enemy and not to just sit back and watch the battle. Sometimes I think we just forget the mission of Christ and we just sit back in our eternal security and drink sweet tea as we wait for the end.

Unfortunately it can be easy for us to find every reason why we can't do things for Christ but when it comes to doing things that do not bring glory to the Kingdom we have no problem charging forward. Doesn't that sound a little backwards? I mean He only died for us, right? He is the one being who holds the key to our eternal life and yet some of us can't even bare to give Him two hours out of the week that He has given us. Imagine if your children did not do what you asked of them. They would be disciplined and restricted from all kinds of things. But we serve a God who still blesses us beyond our disobedience and insolence.

Are we just scared that we won't be able to have the life we want if we live life by the Word? Well, let me tell you, God knows what we want better than we do and His plans for our life will guide us right to our true heart's desire and to true happiness. What we think we want and need could lead us to destruction and we don't even know it. The Word of God is the perfect guide and, if you just follow the instructions left for us in it, it will relieve lots of pressure from our minds thinking that we are supposed to figure it all out. We just have to focus on the Lord and He will take care of the rest.

The Scriptures help us to find what gifts we have and who we are in Christ. It is our spiritual nourishment that can keep us on the narrow path of righteousness. Our life should be our worship not just our singing on Sunday morning. I implore you to dig deeper in the

Word, find your calling/purpose and be a doer of the Word. Not just a hearer.

Study Verse-

"For many are called, but few are chosen."
Matthew 22:14 NLT

"The Lord directs our steps, so why try to understand everything along the way?"
Proverbs 20:24 NLT

CHOICE CHALLENGE #9:

Making the Choice to Find a Mentor

Who do you hang around with? Are there people around you who are going in the same direction? Is there someone who is on a track you would like to be on in a few years? Do you see God moving in your interactions? I hope so. Relationships can be wonderful and very fulfilling, they can also be damaging and draining. It is ever important to be mindful of our surrounding population.

In our walk toward the God goal set before us, it is vital to have godly influence from people who are heading toward Christ. Which brings us to our challenge, "Making the Choice to Find a Mentor".

Having a mature Christian person around you that can be followed in faith and behaviors is a great way to jointly walk in a righteous path and secure accountability. If you are frequently hanging around the same sinful people and participating in the same old activities on a constant basis, than your growth in the Lord has probably been stunted. We have to find people that are walking a mature walk with God and spend time with them a couple times a week. Pretty soon, they will rub off on you and you will be walking a mature walk too.

Like we addressed in *Apples and Oranges,* the people that you surround yourself with will ultimately decide what kind of person you appear to be to others. If you are a Christian, you shouldn't be spending a lot of time with someone who makes a sinful atmosphere in his or her dwelling place. That will only assist you in backsliding, especially if you are a baby Christian. It's fine to have friends of all kinds; we just need to know where to draw the line. It's smart to create a circle around yourself of different people. We should have some folks who minister to us and some we minister to. It's valuable for us to have mentors and a couple people you can mentor. If you have someone in your life you admire, it will push you to get to where you want to be. Make sure you have people around you who will be honest and hold you accountable. That is vital in order to stay focused and to keep your Christian walk pure. And, though it can seem hard to rearrange your surroundings, the payoff is more than worth it.

"So you will walk in the way of good men and keep to the paths of the righteous." Proverbs 2:20 NASB

Challenge :

Write down the names of your true friends. Next to their names write down some benefits of the relationship and what may be a hindrance. Evaluate your list to see if you have a balance in your friend circle. If not, think what relationships do not honor God that you may need to weed out and figure out what you need to do to incorporate more God honoring friendships. Balance is key. Pray that the Lord will send you Godly friends and counsel. Prayer is always our best weapon.

Prayer:

Lord Jesus, thank You for always molding me. Today I choose to surrender my relationships to You. Lord, protect me from wrong relationship and give me wisdom and discernment to know the difference between a sheep and a wolf in sheep's clothing. Lord, send me a godly mentor that will point me in Your direction. Prepare me for the work that You are going to do in me. In Jesus Name , AMEN!

My Journey

What relationships have I allowed to stunt my growth in Christ?

What godly people in my life have potential to be a godly mentor for me?

What person can I mentor?

What mature Christian can I sharpen my iron with?

Discussion Questions

What did I learn about myself in this section?

What Scriptures stood out to me in this section?

What life application do I intend to implement with the discoveries that I have made?

Journaling Page

_____

_____

_____

_____

_____

_____

_____

_____

_____

_____

_____

_____

_____

_____

_____

_____

_____

_____

_____

_____

_____

_____

Part 10

Tongue Tying

Now this will be a fairly short chapter, but ever so important. When journeying towards joy, I believe it's crucial to address the issue of what comes from the orifice in our faces. What spills from that space may very well be putting a fog over someone else's joy or maybe even our own. Our words have a weight that they carry with them. We have a choice to send our words out as a burden or as a blessing. Or whether we should send them out at all.

"Holy Cow!!!" I screamed as I swayed down the road in a near tornado one morning on my way to Walmart. My heart raced as if I was running a marathon and I was nearing the end of mile one. I was completely consumed with worry as I neared my children to safety and tried to look totally calm so that they wouldn't totally lose it before we got there. Thank God that the employees at the door were gracious and ushered us to their tornado safe zone in the back of the store. While all of us sat in silence in the storeroom waiting, for the storm to pass, my mind could only focus on what it was going to look like on the other end of the storm. In that silence I could rest a bit, knowing that I didn't have to leave that place of waiting until it was safe to step out. Though I may have sat in a quiet wonder, my heart was able to just be still.

That morning's trauma was great material for what we are about to venture into. Silence. It may sound completely uneventful and underwhelming, but silence is incredibly valuable. It can bring peace. It can cultivate hope. It can bring strength. It can create opportunities. Sadly, for a good portion of us, silence is scary and/or unproductive. Quiet space can make us feel uncomfortable or anxious. We are so trained to think that every second of every day must be filled with noise of some kind, that finding a white space is almost an inconvenience. I struggle with this. When it gets quiet around me, I automatically feel like I've missed something or as if I should be engaged in something. It's extremely hard for busybodies, like myself, to be comfortable in the quiet, rather in actions or conversation.

We may feel entitled to our opinions in dialogue. We may even feel like we need to make our voices heard to the Father. However, I find that when I am still and noiseless, that is when God's will prevails and not my own.

"1For everything there is a season, and a time for every matter under heaven:

"7a time to tear, and a time to sew; a time to keep silence, and a time to speak;"

Ecclesiastes 3:1, 7 ESV

The Dormant Tongue

Throughout my growing up, I have been very active in expressing my right to say what I felt needed to be heard. In my mind, I had come to the conclusion that it was important that people knew where I stood. I had rationalized my efforts of trying to keep myself protected. There was so much in my past that had helped me to come to this. Watching people around me, who seemed to be getting walked on and mistreated and wanting to simply control my environment. Which is a joke, because who are we kidding, we can't control anything. And now, in hindsight, I see how all of my yammering and "expressions of self" got me in trouble and may have held me in a diluted reality for an extended period of time. Maybe, like many others, I concluded that being silent was a sign of weakness. As if I was showing my strength by voicing my stance.

It's safe to say that we allow our tongues to get us into plenty of trouble. Whether to our own detriment or to the detriment of another. The movement of our tongues may seem harmless, but the sound that streams from our faces can make or break people, opportunities, feelings, peace in an environment, and do irreversible damage. *"Death and life are in the power of the tongue, and those who love it will eat its fruits"* Proverbs 18:21

ESV. This is why we are here. The lack of self-control in our speech may be putting a wall between us, and the joy that we have been given. Our vocal expressions may have created an atmosphere around us that is not conducive to the presence of the Holy Spirit who bears the joy that we take part in.

Honestly, there is tremendous strength found in learning to be quiet. Surrendering our right to be heard provides opportunity for humility to grow and our spirit to be strengthened. When we walk through the door of silence, our attempts can rest, leaving room for God to work. Choosing to be silent could quite well be one of the most difficult choices to make. Especially for someone like me, who has opinions on just about everything and loves dialogue. Which is totally natural. Humans love to be heard. Particularly when they feel offended, under-minded, challenged or ignored. However, our natural instincts are what get us into trouble. It's much more beneficial for us to reserve our opinions and statements, and stand in waiting until it is safe to step out.

A tongue that lies dormant is often a tongue that honors the Lord. Holding on to silence when your flesh wants to have its way will keep us from sin. Not letting your opinion be known is sometimes exactly what the conversation needs. Not allowing your flesh's desire to gossip surface is sometimes all it takes to stop a rumor. Waiting on the Lord to avenge you is much safer than letting the sword in your mouth have its way. There will always be fewer casualties when someone chooses silence.

Study Verse - Proverbs10:19-21 NIV

""Sin is not ended by multiplying words, but the prudent hold their tongues. The tongue of the righteous is choice silver but the heart of the wicked is of little value. The lips of the righteous nourish many, but fools die for lack of sense."

Words That Welcome

Moving on to actual sound coming from our mouths.

Our words can make or break situations and people. Whether it be statements of truth or not, they can leave a residue with a person that can last for years. I remember things that have been said to me that have totally shaped who I am today. Both in good ways and in not so good ways. One instance in particular was when I auditioned for a choir as a teen, after years of singing, and was told that my voice wasn't quite ready to be a part of a choir. That moment in time stuck with me for years. It made me afraid to try out for anything. Not just singing, but all kinds of things. I sat in a state of self-doubt for a really long time. You see, the words that come out of our mouths can chisel away at people and their spirits, whether it be intentional or not.

For this reason, it is especially important for us to pay close attention to the nouns, verbs and adjectives that we allow to escape our mouths.

"Gracious words are like a honeycomb, sweetness to the soul and health to the body." Proverbs 16:24 ESV

What we express in word can open doors or shut them. As carriers of grace, the words that we extend should be words that are welcoming and not deflecting. The great goal is to live out the Gospel and the love that fuels it. Our welcoming words offer opportunity for the love of Christ to enter in and change lives. Bringing healing and unleashing JOY.

"The thoughts of the wicked are an abomination to the Lord, but gracious words are pure" Proverbs 15:26 ESV

Each communication we have with people is a chance to encourage and allow God to enlighten. Taking this for granted is what gets us in those situations where we wish we could pull words back into our mouths. If we approach our interactions as opportunities, our words can bless and build up, rather than tear down.

Study Verse - Ephesians 4:29-32 NIV

"Do not let any unwholesome talk come out of your mouths, but only what is helpful for building others up according to their needs, that it may benefit those who listen. And do not grieve the Holy Spirit of God, with whom you were sealed for the day of redemption. Get rid of all bitterness, rage and anger, brawling and slander, along with every form of malice. Be kind and

compassionate to one another, forgiving each other, just as in Christ God forgave you."

Words Digested

OK....so now that we've talked about words we put out, what about the words we take in?

Like I said previously, I have allowed some words to take root and do some damage that held me back for a number of years. From my example, you have seen what can happen, but I am sure that you have your own memories that shaped you. Someone has said something to you; maybe as a child or maybe as an adult, that has stained you in some way. You have carried a weight of words around with you for who knows how long. You can recall exactly what was said, how it was said, and what day it was said. It's imprinted on your brain like an embossment, you wish it would just leave but there's something in you that has just held on to it.

Well guess what? You don't have to keep it. You can unstitch that monogrammed lie. You can chose to not digest the words that have made you sick all this time. The lies that have been uttered to us have only the power we give them. The hurtful things said to us, although they hurt, do not need to take up unwelcomed residence in our lives.

Today we are going to decide to only digest the TRUTH and the lovely and nothing more because the rest can make us sick.

"Finally, brothers and sisters, whatever is true, whatever is noble, whatever is right, whatever is pure, whatever is lovely, whatever is admirable—if anything is excellent or praiseworthy—think about such things."
Philippians 4:8 NIV

We have the choice of what we want to do with what is spoken to us. We can take it in and allow it to make a home in our hearts or we can release it back to where it came from. We should not willfully digest the lies and destructive statements that want so desperately to make a home in us. When we do, our hearts are made vulnerable to more attacks of the enemy. He is at the heart of every lie.

"You belong to your father, the devil, and you want to carry out your father's desires. He was a murderer from the beginning, not holding to the truth, for there is no truth in him. <u>When he lies, he speaks his native language, for he is a liar and the father of lies.</u>" John 8:44 NIV

The enemy knows that all he has is deception. He knows that the truth of the living God can set us free, so he breaks out his arsenal of lies, loads them up, and points them right at us. He also knows that once we have the truth, his lies cannot stand and his intentions crumble in the presence of God's powerful truth. We are in no way obligated to buy any lie that he presents to us. When we take up the Sword of Truth and stand firm, the lies of the enemy are defeated and powerless.

Every word that presents itself to us is not meant for us. Measure every word that presents itself against the Word of God. Digest the truth and trash the lie.

Study Verse - Ephesians 4:27 NIV

"and do not give the devil a foothold."

CHOICE CHALLENGE #10:

Making the Choice to Be Silent and Speak Life-Giving Words

I don't know about you, but I struggle with taming my tongue. It is something I bring before the Lord on a daily basis. I literally have to hold my mouth shut by the end of the day. It may be best for some of us to carry this challenge for a few extra days for the safety of those we interact with at least.

This challenge is going to be twofold.

Part 1: For the first part of this challenge, we are going to practice the lost art of saying nothing when we want nothing more than anything to rattle off all that we feel needs to be said. We are "Making the Choice to Be Silent". I know that this seems like an impossible feat for some of us, especially in the moments when we are in complete opposition with someone. You may have to keep yourself from jumping out of your skin a few times, but this will be well worth it. This challenge will show you things about yourself and others that you never realized were there.

Let's pause before every response, reaction, or comment today. Take a moment of silence for the words that you want to say and really think on the necessity for them to make an exit. Because truth be told, a good portion of the words we spout off, are unnecessary and many times unwanted. Our silence shows people that they matter more than our opinion and offers the Father space to speak to us and through us. If it helps, write down the words that you want to say so that you don't feel like you will explode from not being able to let them out.

Today I encourage you to bless those around you with silence and watch how much you learn about yourself. If it gets hard to just keep your mouth closed, pinch your lips closed with your fingers and just nod your head up and down so that they know that you are listening. It works every time!

Part 2: For the next part of this challenge we are going to make a choice regarding what we do when we unleash the sword in our mouths. Remember that old lie we used to believe, "sticks and stones may break my bones, but words can never harm me"? What a crock!!!! That is in no way true. Words can do so much damage. They can separate families, cause division and breaking down the human spirit. Words can also be full of life. They can build up confidence, encourage growth, give love, or share truth.

We are "Making the Choice to Speak Life-Giving Words." This is another difficult one. It can really be a mountain climb depending on the environment you spend most of your time in. That opinionated coworker, the micromanaging supervisor, the hyperactive child, the unsupportive spouse, and the list can go on forever. Each of these life happenings can be a lighter to your wick if you let them. What if we chose to do the unexpected and put out the flame with quenching words? Words that can calm and bring peace instead of causing anger and resentment. What if we speak encouraging words to the people around us? *"Gentle words are a tree of life, a deceitful tongue crushes the spirit."* Proverbs 15:4. Sometimes all it takes is one encouraging word to change the course of someone's day or even his/her life. Words hold the power of life or death. Let's make a conscious effort to speak gentle words no matter what, no matter who.

Prayer:

Lord, thank You for Your constant grace and protection. Please forgive us where we have failed. We release our tongues to You today. Give us hearts like Yours so that our mouths will pour out love and lifegiving words to those around us. Help us to use self-control in moments where we feel challenged or offended. Let Your Holy Spirit consume our thoughts and surround us so that we can share His peace with others. In Jesus Name, Amen!

My Journey

What areas do I struggle tying down my tongue?

What words spoken by others have I allowed to break down God's truth in my life?

Where do I struggle to surrender my speech to Christ?

How can I better use my words to uplift others and myself?

Discussion Questions

What did I learn about myself in this section?

What Scriptures stood out to me in this section?

What life application do I intend to implement with the discoveries that I have made?

Journaling Page

Part 11

Don't Forget Love

I hate to even admit it, but here we are in our last chapter (pauses to wipe tears). This has been an incredible journey so far. An expedition that has been one of discomfort, enlightenment, struggle and delightful truth. I pray that up until this point you have seen God bring you closer to Him and the lasting joy that He has given to you. In this final chapter, we are going to hit the refresh button on something that many of us have let fade a little. LOVE! The epicenter of our faith and our faith walk.

We have used the word *Love* extremely flippantly in many cases.

I love ice cream! (and I do!)

I love dogs!

I love Target!

I love sleep! (I mean…..just saying.)

That last one may very well be legit and sincere for most of us, but for the most part, we have diluted the word *Love* and made it fairly underwhelming in many ways. This is so very ill-fitting when we view love from the Father's perspective.

Love: an intense feeling of deep affection

Agapao (Greek for Love): to be fond of, to love dearly

Loving Who God loves….

The Lord's greatest commandment is, *"This is My commandment, that you love one another, just as I have loved you."* John 15:12 NASB. This seems like such a simple but important commandment. However it also seems as though it is one of the hardest commandments to abide by at times.

Sometimes we think that because we are extending ourselves to love the people around us that we are loving everyone like we are supposed to. We give and give and give of ourselves and think that we have accomplished all the loving that we were meant to do. But there is one thing that we leave out. We sometimes forget to love ourselves. How can we ever forget to love ourselves? We have God living in us at this very moment, so we should love ourselves. Somehow we can forget to invest time for thoughts regarding the love we have for ourselves very easily. We get so wrapped up in doing and doing and doing for everyone else or perhaps doing absolutely nothing, that we forget that we even exist. In that cyclone of exterior thinking, comes a breaking point when you realize that you have hit the bottom and have not loved yourself enough. We usually realize it after someone has brought it to our attention or possibly after the first couple of meltdowns in the grocery store.

As a mother, I know it can be incredibly hard to gauge when it's time to pull back and take some "self-fill up" time. At times, I realize it a little too late and find myself lock in a closet having heart palpitations (I do not recommend waiting until you hit that level to pull back and get filled up.). The point is, if I would stop for a moment and realize that my creator loved me enough to breathe life into me, I could open my heart up to love myself enough to take care of who my Father loves through the way I take care of my mind, body and soul.

How can we possibly love the people around us properly, if we have no love for ourselves? Better yet, how can we know how to love those around us if we don't know how our Father loves us? We are in spiritual warfare and one of the devil's best weapons is to get us to hate ourselves so that it is easier to get us to hate other people. *"Hatred stirs up strife, But love covers all transgressions."* Proverbs 10:12 NASB. He knows that hurting people hurt other people. It's a chain reaction. Our best weapon is Jesus and He IS LOVE! *"For God so loved the world, that He gave His only begotten Son.....* " John 3:16 NASB.

Though the world we live in can help us to harbor hate for ourselves and forget who loves us, maybe it will do us good to remember that we are loved by the Most High. We are loved by the creator so much that He gave up His only son. We are loved so much that He continues to provide even when we are disobedient and hateful. We are loved just how we are. Broken, bruised, arrogant, addicted, selfish and sinful, yet He still loves us. We have to choose to love what He loves, including self, because our flesh is not naturally filled with the love of the Lord. Choose to love yourself as He has loved you. Only then can the healing begin and we can love others.

Study Verse – 1 John 4:8 NASB

"The one who does not love does not know God, for God is love."

Loving People Where They Are

I have mentioned before how we can have a tendency to allow the lifestyles of people around us affect our happiness to a certain point. That being said, today I will touch on a similar topic from a different angle.

When settling a sibling disagreement in my home, we usually bring them together and make them come to amendment. While we are hashing out the details of what transpired in the first place, the details tend to get foggy and the blame is always shifty. When I say things like, " You should not do that," usually the response is, "But they did 'this' to me." They seem almost disgusted that I don't understand why they have taken the actions they have in response to the other child. While they stand and state their case for why they have not shown love for their sibling, in my head I'm thinking, "What if Christ gave according to what we do?" We would be bankrupt.

When we have people in our lives that we don't exactly feel are leading the best life, it's very easy to slip into judgment mode. All of a sudden we forget all that we have ever done or may be still doing. We start trying to figure out ways to fix them and get them on track. Sometimes we even have the audacity to preach to them and then cut them off, totally forgetting about grace and mercy, and the abundance of both that we ourselves have received. Where would we be if our Father had that same reaction to the mistakes we've made? He would have never sent His son to die on the cross and we would be on the fast track to hell.

We have all been called to LOVE one another above all else. We have not been called to assume the role of God, condemn, cast out, or regulate one another. *"My command is this: Love each other as I have loved you."* John 15:12 NIV. There is joy in loving those around us. Loving them through service, kindness and by being the example rather than trying to constantly correct them.

Your love alone will lead them to Christ not your badgering.

Don't get me wrong, I know it can be hard to see people we care about going off the deep end without trying to throw them a lifeline, but have you ever thought that your love could be all the lifeline they need. Our lifeline can often look a lot like control and condemnation, making it difficult for the people we are trying to "help" to see the love of Christ and the redemption attached to the Cross He carried. Just knowing that someone is going to love them no matter where they are in life, is all they may need. God loves us at every stage of life, and though He may not love the things we do all the time, He will always love us and be waiting with open arms. Right now our world is crying for people who will just love them right where they are. Without all the rules and regulations sometimes associated with religion, just LOVE. I believe we are all called to love and serve one another, right now!

Study Verse - Luke 6:35-36 NIV

"But love your enemies, do good to them, and lend to them without expecting to get anything back. Then your reward will be great, and you will be children of the Most High, because he is kind to the ungrateful and wicked. Be merciful, just as your Father is merciful"

Serving Someone Other Than Me...

It's so easy for us to get caught up in the "me, my, I" world when living here on earth. Especially when all we see on TV, in magazines, and stores that we need this and that, and how we need to please ourselves. Nowhere in the good book (the Bible) does it say, "Please yourself and life will be good". That is because pleasing ourselves is actually counterproductive when it comes to living a joyful life. Having the latest car, biggest house or hottest pair of Jimmy Choo shoes is not going to keep a smile on our face. That temporary smile just might burst into tears when the bill comes. Also, most times this type of behavior leads to addiction and/or depression. The reason is because you are trying so hard to get happiness through finding different ways of pleasing yourself and none of them are working. So you either get frustrated and then depressed or you look for relief in other things like drugs or alcohol. All the while you don't realize that if you focus that energy used on yourself to help someone else, you will slowly but surely began to find joy you didn't even know you could have. The small bit of joy that comes from pleasing yourself doesn't last but the joy from serving others last for a long time.

If being a Christian is about being Christ like, we must consider what Christ was like. Christ served everyone whether it was washing feet or through miracles. *"For even the Son of Man did not come to be served, but to serve…" Mark 10:45(NIV)*. Being able to give or serve someone else is a gift and will bring joy to both the person serving and the person receiving. Looking past our own needs to see the needs of others will also help us appreciate what we already have. You can't be happy with where you are unless you can see how far others have to go. Take the time to invest in someone else and see how much better you feel.

Study Verse - Ephesians 6:7 NIV

"Serve wholeheartedly, as if you were serving the Lord, not people,"

CHOICE CHALLENGE #11:

Making the Choice to Love

Here we are at our final challenge together. A little bitter sweet, huh? I know, I didn't want this to end either. This challenge is by far one of the most important of all. This challenge will force us to reach into dark places and walk on paths we thought we would never walk. To walk the very same paths that our King Jesus walked; paths that take us to the broken and hurting, paths that will take us to forgiveness and grace and paths that will take us to healing and freedom. For us. For others.

Our challenge, "Making the Choice to Love", can swing open the doors of joy faster than just about anything. Reaching out with the love that we have been given to offer the same gifts that we have been given.

"Beloved, let us love one another, for love is from God, and whoever loves has been born of God and knows God." 1 John 4:7 ESV

For this challenge, let's take the road we haven't taken in love. Let's love the unlovable and choose love in the circumstances where love is not the natural first choice. When we choose love first, we lay down our agenda and choose the God agenda that always prevails and satisfies. I encourage you to go and outdo yourself in love. Love God and people more that you have ever loved before. Create a strategy if you need to. Write notes with loving words on them that you can share, or just as reminders to yourself. Pray often that the Holy Spirit would fill you with His love so that you will have what you need to give.

Our Father is so in love with us and we all deserve to know that. So let's go out and be that love that He so desperately wants to give.

"So we have come to know and to believe the love that God has for us. God is love, and whoever abides in love abides in God, and God abides in him. By this is love perfected with us, so that we may have confidence for the day of judgment, because as he is so also are we in this world." 1 John 4:16-17 ESV

Prayer:

Lord Jesus, You have loved me before I knew what love was. Thank You for Your never-ending love and affections for me. Please show me how to be love to others and how to express Your love to them. Lord, help me to never forget the love that You have for me and what You have done to show me. Renew my heart, Father, so that Your love can dwell in me continuously. In Jesus name, Amen!

My Journey

Am I struggling to love myself?

What areas do I struggle to be love to someone else?

What areas do I put limits on my love?

How can I demonstrate the love of Christ in my daily life?

What has stopped me from extending sincere Christ like love to those around me?

How can I better serve the people in my life?

Discussion Questions

What did I learn about myself in this section?

What Scriptures stood out to me in this section?

What life application do I intend to implement with the discoveries that I have made?

Journaling Page

_____

_____

_____

_____

_____

_____

_____

_____

_____

_____

_____

_____

_____

_____

_____

_____

_____

_____

_____

_____

_____

_____

Conclusion

Pheww....We made it!!!! We survived!

Are you OK? You still like me right?

I'm so proud of you friend! You have battled it out with me and made it to the end. I'm sure that some of this experience was tough but I know that God will use every ounce of what He has revealed to you throughout this for your good and His glory.

We have traveled through many areas of life in this journey: past, present, and future. We took some unexpected turns and some revealing looks into ourselves, looking for truth, looking for resolve, looking for what's always been there. Christ's everlasting JOY!

My own journey has brought me to the revelation that *The Truth About Happiness* is, happiness is a bi-product of the real stuff, JOY. Without the sustaining truth of God's Word being at the forefront of my life, I can't really be in possession of either. I can only possess the counterfeits. The Gospel makes way for us to tap into a well of satisfaction. When I resolve that through Jesus all my needs can be found, my life can be open to experience the fullness of the inheritance I have in Him.

I know that this has been quite an emotional journey. We have walked through some tough topics and hit a few sore spots I'm sure. None of it was in vain. To God be the glory!!

I pray that you have seen God's heart for you in this journey. His Word is truly our key to it all. His truth balances it all out. His Word breaks down every lie and clears up confusion that keeps us from experiencing Him fully. We can have the joy that He has given us because He has already paid for that gift, wrapped it in salvation, and given it to us with great pleasure and generosity. It's up to us to make the choice to unwrap the gift. Make the choice daily my friend!

See you on our next journey!

Love,

J. E. Berry

"pray without ceasing." *1 Thessalonians 5:17*

My Journey

What parts of this process have impacted my life the most?

How has my life been changed through this journey?

Who can I invite to take this journey?

Discussion Questions

What did I learn about myself in this process?

What Scriptures stood out to me in this journey?

What life application do I intend to implement with the discoveries that I have made overall?

Journaling Page

Reference

Invitation to Salvation

Dear friend, you are in the right place. If you have never professed and known Jesus Christ as the Savior and Lord of your life, today is a great day to walk toward Him and allow Him to change your life forever. We are all sinners and are in need of a Savior.

Scripture allows us to see how we have been redeemed and why God chose to save us from an eternity without Him in death.

"For God so loved the world, that he gave his only Son, that whoever believes in him should not perish but have eternal life. For God did not send his Son into the world to condemn the world, but in order that the world might be saved through him. Whoever believes in him is not condemned, but whoever does not believe is condemned already, because he has not believed in the name of the only Son of God." John 3:16-18 ESV

"for all have sinned and fall short of the glory of God, and are justified by his grace as a gift, through the redemption that is in Christ Jesus, whom God put forward as a propitiation by his blood, to be received by faith. This was to show God's righteousness, because in his divine forbearance he

had passed over former sins." Romans 3:23-25 ESV

"For the wages of sin is death, but the free gift of God is eternal life in Christ Jesus our Lord." Romans 6:23 ESV

I invite you to call upon Jesus and ask Him to take over the life that He has given you. I invite you to step into the place of honor and freedom that was paid for you by the blood of Jesus on the Cross, many years ago. I invite you to walk in the forgiveness that has been freely offered to you by God the Father. Don't waste another minute. The love of God has brought you here and His love wants nothing more than to set you free from condemnation and the weight of this world.

"For with the heart one believes and is justified, and with the mouth one confesses and is saved. For the Scripture says, "Everyone who believes in him will not be put to shame." For there is no distinction between Jew and Greek; for the same Lord is Lord of all, bestowing his riches on all who call on him. For "everyone who calls on the name of the Lord will be saved." Romans 10:10-13 ESV If you believe that you are ready to allow Jesus into your heart and your life, below there is a prayer of salvation for you. Take some time to quiet your heart and reach out to God in this new way so that He can renew your heart and spirit.

Prayer of Salvation:

God, I know that I have sinned. Today I am coming to You asking for Your forgiveness. I confess that Jesus Christ is my Savior, my Lord, and my only way back to You. Jesus I give You my life and my heart to be made new. I am choosing to put my trust in You today and always. In Jesus name, Amen!

_____
Sign

Date:_____   Time:_____

Welcome to the family! You will never be the same!

My advice to you now is that you find a local Bible teaching church of fellow believers and get connected and cared for. Study God's Word and allow Him to do a great work in you from the inside out.

Bible Versions Used

All Scripture was sourced from the following versions:

New American Standard Bible (NASB), first published (complete Bible) 1971

English Standard Version (ESV), first published 2001

New Living Translation (NLT), first published 1979

New International Version (NIV/NIVUK), first published 1973

New King James Version (NKJV) first published 1996

Definitions

All English terms were retrieved from:

"change", ahdictionary.com, 2016, https://ahdictionary.com/word/search.html?q=change

"choose", ahdictionary.com, 2016, https://ahdictionary.com/word/search.html?q=choose

"defeated", thefreedictionary.com, 2016, http://www.thefreedictionary.com/defeated   "denial",

ahdictionary.com, 2016,
https://ahdictionary.com/word/search.html?q=denial

"error", ahdictionary.com, 2016,
https://ahdictionary.com/word/search.html?q=error

"fear", ahdictionary.com, 2016
https://ahdictionary.com/word/search.html?q=feaR

"happy", google.com, 2015
https://www.google.com/?gws_rd=ssl#q=happy+defini
tion

"love", google.com, 2016,
https://www.google.com/?gws_rd=ssl#q=love

"mistake", ahdictionary.com, 2016,
https://ahdictionary.com/word/search.html?q=mistake

"rejected", google.com, 2016,
https://www.google.com/?gws_rd=ssl#q=rejected

"rejection", google.com, 2016,
https://www.google.com/?gws_rd=ssl#q=rejection

"repent", ahdictionary.com , 2016,
https://ahdictionary.com/word/search.html?q=repent

"rescued", google.com, 2015,
https://www.google.com/?gws_rd=ssl#q=rescued+defi
nition

"saved", google.com, 2015,
https://www.google.com/?gws_rd=ssl#q=saved+defini

tion

"selfish", www.merriam-webster.com ,2016,
http://www.merriam-webster.com/dictionary/selfish

"source" google.com, 2015,
https://www.google.com/?gws_rd=ssl#q=source

"truth", ahdictionary.com, 2016,
https://ahdictionary.com/word/search.html?q=truth

"wisdom", ahdictionary.com , 2016,
https://ahdictionary.com/word/search.html?q=wisdom

All Greek or Hebrew terms were retrieved from:

"agapao", Strong, *The New Strong's Exhaustive Concordance of the Bible,* Nashville, TN: Thomas Nelson, 1990, pg. 1 (Greek)

"sofia", google.com, 2016,
https://www.google.com/?gws_rd=ssl#q=wisdom+in+greek